Get the simple things right first. Low-cost public health interventions have the potential to stop this pandemic in its tracks. While these measures may seem like common sense, in fact, they have to be learned. This text is a great place to start that learning.

High tech, scientific advances in therapeutics, and vaccines will come. In the meantime, the main things are the plain things, simple day-to-day modifications in lifestyle can stop contagion and save lives. This text details these, with practicalities and rationales for their implementation.

**Dr. John Campbell, PhD RN, retired nursing professor, YouTube channel with 737k subscribers**

What a great game plan to help us navigate through this pandemic. I'll run with this!

**Franco Harris, former NFL player, NFL Hall of Fame member**

Medical concepts, like Rocket Science, are always hard to translate into understandable and actionable terms. As my fellow epidemiologists—disease detectives—struggle to uncover the secrets of COVID19, Skills offers an approachable blueprint for action that all of us on the planet should heed. An equivalent of a naval aviator or astronaut's checklist for understanding the critical steps necessary to combat COVID.

**Captain J.M. Linenger, Medical Corps, U.S. Navy (ret.) NASA astronaut/Mir Cosmonaut STS-64, STS-81, Mir 23, STS 84 physician (MD), epidemiologist (PhD), and author of *Off the Planet***

This book not only gave me the information I needed to understand our role in responding to the pandemic, but it is a practical tool to, "Love your neighbor as you love yourself." I appreciate the expertise and the care that went into this valuable work!

**Rev. Dr. Joel C. Hunter, faith-based community organizer, retired pastor, and chairman, Community Resource Network**

As health care professionals explaining the complexities of the pandemic to non-medical professionals can be daunting especially because of the complexity and the changing nature of the virus. Citizens continue to question the policies and guidelines that are being put in place because they seriously affect our everyday lives. This book does an excellent job in taking the mystery out of COVID -19 for non-health professionals by putting the virus and the science in terms people can understand. I encourage anyone who has questions about this pandemic and those that are even a little bit skeptical about the seriousness of the virus spend some time with this valuable educational tool.

**Deborah L. Arms PhD RN, Ohio Nurses Association**

It's much more detailed than the safety information from corporate or the CDC. The question-and-answer sections are particularly useful for testing our understanding of how this pandemic spreads.

**Joe Beddal, sandwich shop owner in State College, PA**

Nature will have its way, with storms, floods, and disease. That does not mean it has to win. The key is to have a plan. This book offers a roadmap for the COVID-19 pandemic and for future outbreaks; events that disproportionately impact communities of color and the disadvantaged.

**Lt. Gen. Russel Honoré, USA (ret.), author of *Survival: How Being Prepared Can Keep You and Your Family Safe***

# SKILLS TO OBSTRUCT PANDEMICS

## How to protect yourself and your community from COVID-19 and similar infections

Frank E. Ritter, PhD • Amanda C. Clase, PhD
Stephanie Leigh Harvill, BFA MEd • Martin K.-C. Yeh, PhD
Renuka E. Joseph, MS • Jeffrey J. Oury, MD
Jacob D. Oury, BS • Edward J. Glantz, MBA PhD
Alexis Fenstermacher, BSN RN • Mathieu Brener, PhD
James J. James, MD DrPH MHA

SUNBURY PRESS

Mechanicsburg, PA USA

Published by Sunbury Press, Inc.
Mechanicsburg, PA USA

**www.sunburypress.com**

For information about special discounts for bulk purchases, please contact Sunbury Press Orders Dept. at (855) 338-8359 or orders@sunburypress.com.

To request one of our authors for speaking engagements or book signings, please contact Sunbury Press Publicity Dept. at publicity@sunburypress.com.

FIRST SUNBURY PRESS EDITION:  December 2020

Set in Noto Serif | Interior design by Crystal Devine | Cover by Kean Zekić | Edited by Abigail Henson.

Publisher's Cataloging-in-Publication Data
Names: Ritter, Frank E., author | et al, authors.
Title: Skills to obstruct pandemics : how to protect yourself and your community from COVID-19 and similar infections / Frank E. Ritter, et al.
Description: First trade paperback edition. | Mechanicsburg, PA : Sunbury Press, 2020.
Summary: This book teaches knowledge and skills to help interrupt the transmission of COVID-19 caused by the SARS-CoV-2 virus. These skills are also applicable to other respiratory pathogens and will also generally help decrease the spread of most infections.
Identifiers: ISBN 978-1-620064-37-5 (softcover).
Subjects: MEDICAL / Infectious Diseases | MEDICAL / Epidemiology | HEALTH & FITNESS / Diseases / Contagious | HEALTH & FITNESS / Reference | SOCIAL SCIENCE / Disease & Health Issues.

Product of the United States of America
0  1  1  2  3  5  8  13  21  34  55

*Continue the Enlightenment!*

# Experts Consulted Who Approve this Material

This information was approved by:

**Tina Bauermeister, MS RDN, LD**
Registered Dietitian Nutritionist (the nutrition and vitamins pages)

**Amanda C. Clase, PhD**
Associate Research Professor, Applied Research Laboratory, Penn State

**Alexis (Lex) Fenstermacher, BSN RN**
Medical Surgical Nurse, Penn State/UPMC Presbyterian Hospital

**Chris Garrison, PhD RN CNE CHSE**
Associate Teaching Professor of Nursing, Director of the Simulation Lab
College of Nursing, Penn State

**James J. James, MD DrPH MHA**
Chief Executive Officer
Society for Disaster Medicine and Public Health

**Renuka Elizabeth Joseph, ScM, PhD candidate**
Molecular, Cellular, and Integrative Bioscience program
Penn State

**Dan Kirkpatrick Col, USAF (Ret.) RN MSN**
Former Mayor of Fairborn, OH; Past President, Ohio Nurses Association

**Jeffrey J. Oury, MD**
West Virginia University School of Medicine

**Matt Owens, MD**
Rural Health Program, Sanford Medical School (the mask section and
the wellness section)

**Jose A. Soto, PhD**
Associate Professor of Psychology, licensed clinical psychologist
Penn State (wellness section)

**IN MEMORY OF FREDRICK RYANS** who helped on this project while doing his PhD, and dedicated to all those who have had their lives turned upside-down yet cheerfully provide healthcare to the public, working from home while providing daycare, and those hard-working folks continuing to make products, stock shelves, take orders, drive trucks, and make deliveries.

# Table of Contents

# Introduction

This book teaches knowledge and skills to help interrupt the transmission of COVID-19 caused by the SARS-CoV-2 virus. These skills are also applicable to other respiratory pathogens and will also generally help decrease the spread of most infections.

This book is based on a comprehensive online tutor to educate the community about the science and steps we can all take to help reduce the pandemic (StopTheSpread.health). We started to create the tutor in early March 2020 when we saw that there was going to be a pandemic. The coming storm was visible in foreign news reports and first-person videos on Reddit and other news sources.

We are a team based at Penn State who work on computer-based tutoring and theories of learning. We have been joined by two medical doctors, a virologist, a nurse, a bioterrorism expert, and a public health doctor who have contributed prose, comments, and general advice. We have had the contents checked by another doctor, two nurses, a nutritionist, and a clinical psychologist.

The learning theory we use is based on learning declarative information (facts) and then proceduralizing it (turning the facts into skills). The declarative information needed to fight this pandemic is more complex than can be fully covered in a 2-minute TV interview or a single poster. The book thus covers extensive declarative information and then gives readers questions and exercises to help make the knowledge more proceduralized.

The expected tutor and book time is one to three hours. There are many quizzes for practice and mastery learning. If you follow the **Read/Learn More**: notes, you can learn even more. These are available as an online set at **http://StopTheSpread.health/URLs**, which hosts all the links in this book. You can also choose instead to look at single sections and skip around. This time may seem like a long time. This length is required because the material is comprehensive and because the knowledge requires practice and thought. If the content is too long for you, try breaking it up into smaller chunks, looking at single sections, and feeling free to jump around. Many topics are self-contained. You can also skim or skip the quizzes, but you will not learn the material as well. The book assumes you want to learn a lot. Information can change rapidly in this area. We will put updates and errata on the StopTheSpread.health site You can also use the online tutor if you wish—logins are free!

The book and online tutor are designed for non-medical professionals, for example, Penn State students and the people in their community. The tutorial encompasses multiple types of skills. The scenarios reflect everyday life and strategies that can be used by almost everyone.

The goal of this material is for you to understand how viruses spread and to know what you can do to stop the spread of COVID-19 and similar diseases by protecting yourself and others. You will learn basic microbiology concepts. You will learn strategies to reduce the chance of being infected, and that will help "flatten the curve" by reducing or delaying infections. A one-page summary of the skills to obstruct pandemics is available in Figs. 2.2 and 3.1, as a quiz in Appendix 1, and on the tutor's homepage.

The knowledge and skills in this book should also help stop the spread of other infections, including the flu. And these skills will be useful in the next flu season and the next pandemic if there is one (and they are expected).

Stopping the spread is not political, but rather practical. No one likes to become ill. Changing our behavior to reduce infection and the spread should be seen as practicing the Golden Rule, do onto others as you would have them do on to you. Being a good neighbor has many benefits.

We do not present material on why the pandemic is leading to a considerable amount of suffering and how it could rapidly get even worse if not addressed. Information in this area is readily available. We have curated a website containing descriptions of why this is a serious pandemic; if you have any questions—we do not. This disease has not only mortality (death) but also morbidity (long-lasting damage). [https://stopthespread.health/taking-covid-seriously/]

For learners, the disease is COVID or COVID-19 (COronaVIrus Disease [20]19). The disease is caused by the SARS-CoV-2 virus, which is a type of coronavirus. The book uses these terms somewhat interchangeably, but they are technically different things.

All content and media in this book are created and published for informational purposes only. They are not intended to be a substitute for professional medical or healthcare advice and should not be relied on as health or personal advice.

# Acknowledgments

We need to thank many people and organizations who helped create this book. Dan Kirkpatrick provided numerous comments on style and correctness and provided the idea for this project years before this pandemic. Chris Garrison provided advice on numerous occasions. Prof. William Bahnfleth suggested the material about the virus's life in the air and gave a 20 minute interview to provide initial material. Our panel of experts gave suggestions and helped improve the presenation and correctness. We need to thank the Applied Cognitive Science Lab members for comments, assistance, and numerous discussions on this project. Garrett Barch did an internship working on the tutor and book, including writing a paragraph in Section 4, which helped a lot. Matthew J. Norris did part of his required internship with us. He started out helping run a psychology study and ended up helping prepare this material. Darlene Chassé Ash, Father Richard Baker, Paul Clifford, Catherine Copetas, Steve Croker (several times), Don Donahue, Patrick Dudas, Cara Exten, David Hozza, William Kennedy, Jong Kim, Edward Mays, Trisha McKee, Stellan Ohlsson, Colleen Ritter, Joseph Ritter, Jack Sparks, Sarah Stager, Yvette and Richard Tenney, and Sue Van Vactor provided comments and advice. The College of IST at Penn State, the Applied Research Lab, The Office of Naval Research, and the Defense Health program provided support for the tutor, and ONR and DHP provided support for the D2P tutoring architecture (N00014-15-1-2275; W81XWH-17-C-0002). iStock.com provided some images under their "Support for Covid" campaign, as did some other resource sites noted in the figure sources. Materials, including pictures and text, are generally drawn from creative commons and US Government websites. We would like to thank Korey MacDougall, former ACS Lab member and consultant, for helping maintain the tutoring system. Myeongcheol Hong and Jacob Oury also helped with this maintenance. And thanks go to Abigail Henson, Crystal Devine, and Lawrence Knorr at Sunbury Press for helping turn this into a book.

A portion of the proceeds (12%) of the book will go to the Society for Disaster Medicine and Public Health, where it will help with information dissemination about disaster preparedness. The online tutor is free to use.

# 1

# What Does Flatten the Curve Mean?

## Overview of Book

This book will help decrease your chances of catching infections based on understanding how they are transferred. There are relatively easy ways to decrease the spread of infections by interrupting every step of the process. The chain of infections are shown metaphorically in Fig. 1.1 and taught throughout this book.

This book helps by teaching you how to separate yourself from infectious material and how to protect people around you if you might be or are infectious. This includes how to cough, how to protect yourself from droplets and contaminated surfaces, and how to keep your hands clean.

Infection, in many cases, is a probabilistic danger. Not every situation you run across will have infectious material. In the case of COVID-19, it is hard to tell when someone is infected and transmitting the virus. Not every precaution is necessary, but it is very difficult to know when the precaution is necessary. So, to help reduce the spread, you should apply as many of these skills as often as you can. Sometimes, nothing will have been prevented. Sometimes, you might save yourself, or you might stop yourself from getting infected and infecting someone else you do not know or someone you care about. The more we apply these skills, the sooner the disease rate decreases, and the sooner we can get back to normal. These skills make a real difference [U1.3].

**Fig. 1.1 [U1.1, U1.2]** A row of safety matches shown catching fire, representing the spread of infection.

You cannot see viruses. The people around you may be contagious without having obvious or any symptoms, so you need to take these precautions even if you do not think you are at risk. You might also be infectious, spreading viruses, even if you do not feel sick.

Now is the time to practice. The military, medical personnel, driving instructors, skydivers, pilots, firefighters, and police all practice the skills they need to use before it counts. So, even if you think you are not at risk today, you still want these skills to be second nature. This book will teach you to identify situations that put you at risk, help you practice making the right decisions, equip you with the knowledge about when and how to wash, and many other related skills.

### READ MORE*

**[U1.1]** "Safety Match" by Juan Delcan & Valentina Izaguirre (@Juan_delcan) [https://www.youtube.com/watch?v=oHx_slAQfMM]

**[U1.2]** Juan Delcan on YouTube [https://www.youtube.com/channel/UCRjQVwyyBD2VpX2u5rFdHkw]

**[U1.3]** This is just one example showing that these skills work to fight infection. Additional references are in appropriate sections: Cowling, Benjamin J., Kwok-Hung Chan, Vicky J. Fang, Calvin KY Cheng, Rita OP Fung, Winnie Wai, Joey Sin et al. 2009. "Facemasks and hand hygiene to prevent influenza transmission in households: A cluster randomized trial." Annals of Internal Medicine 151: 437-446. [https://www.researchgate.net/publication/26714438_Facemasks_and_Hand_Hygiene_to_Prevent _Influenza_Transmission_in_Households_A_Cluster_Randomized_Trial]

## Flatten the Curve

Fig. 1.2 shows a match that did not catch the flame and protected the matches on the other side from igniting. You could be that match!

If you are concerned about the COVID-19 pandemic and would like to help on an individual level, you can use this material to practice the ways to protect yourself and thus protect others because you will learn how to stop the transmission.

**Why are we making a big deal about this virus?** The evidence so far suggests that perhaps 80% of the people who get the disease, COVID-19, will have a "mild" illness. But that does not mean people with mild symptoms have it easy. "Mild" includes everything up to pneumonia that does not require hospitalization. Approximately 14% will experience more severe illness, and approximately 6% will experience critical illness (i.e., will require an ICU bed). Of the infected, various estimates have put the death rate of infected cases between 0.2% and 2%—if they are treated. These numbers vary by population and are not yet well understood.

There are typically about 3 hospital beds per 1,000 people in the US, and not all of these are ICU beds. There are other people who would normally

---

\* Resources with indicators like [U1.1] are available as a set at http://StopTheSpread.health/URLs.

**Fig. 1.2 [U1.1]** A row of safety matches illustrating how physical distance can put an end to the flame igniting all the matches when one match steps out of line and stops the spread.

need those beds. If more than 1.5% get COVID-19 at any point in time, then the hospitals can be overwhelmed (unless we get more beds, and we are getting more beds).

The virus spreads exponentially, so the growth rate for infections can be very fast, doubling every few days or every week. As Dr. Fauci, Director of the National Institute of Allergy and Infectious Diseases (NIAID), said, "if it looks like you're overreacting, you're probably doing the right thing." Thus, we need to be very concerned but not unduly afraid.

### READ MORE

**[U1.4]** America's COVID-19 warning system
[https://covidactnow.org/]

**[U1.5]** Fauci: "If it looks like you're overreacting, you're probably doing the right thing"
[https://thehill.com/homenews/sunday-talk-shows/487639-fauci-if-it-looks-like-youre-overreacting
-youre-probably-doing-the]

**[U1.6]** Predictions for COVID-19 infections
[https://projects.fivethirtyeight.com/covid-forecasts/]

## Summary of Flatten the Curve: The Curve Itself

Hospitals and health care facilities usually have capacity. We have seen through numerous reports on TV and the Internet that this is not the case with COVID-19 when it gets out of control.

If enough people are infected at the same time, there will be a peak of sickness that will overwhelm our healthcare resources and perhaps breaking the healthcare workers too. This peak is illustrated in Fig. 1.3.

Flattening the curve, in summary, is doing all that you can at an individual level to slow the spread of infection so that the healthcare system does not become overwhelmed. This flattens the curve of cases, spreading out and reducing the load on the healthcare system at any single point in time.

The higher the exposure rate to an infectious agent, the greater the chance for infection. The less contact and the fewer number of contacts you have, the less likely you are to catch a disease.

Practicing the social distancing and personal hygiene techniques provided in this book can reduce your chances of becoming infected with

# FLATTEN THE CURVE

*Proactively control timing of number of sick, so health care system can take care of all.*

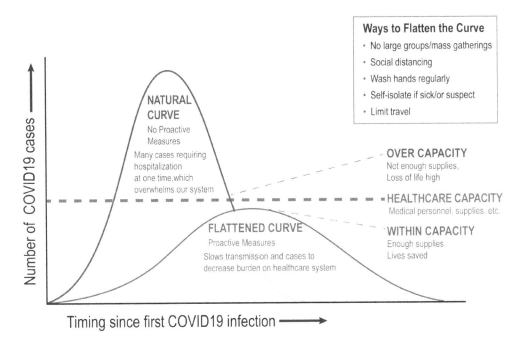

**Ways to Flatten the Curve**
- No large groups/mass gatherings
- Social distancing
- Wash hands regularly
- Self-isolate if sick/or suspect
- Limit travel

**NATURAL CURVE**
No Proactive Measures

Many cases requiring hospitalization at one time, which overwhelms our system

**OVER CAPACITY**
Not enough supplies, Loss of life high

**HEALTHCARE CAPACITY**
Medical personnel, supplies, etc.

**WITHIN CAPACITY**
Enough supplies
Lives saved

**FLATTENED CURVE**
Proactive Measures

Slows transmission and cases to decrease burden on healthcare system

Number of COVID19 cases

Timing since first COVID19 infection

**Fig. 1.3** Reducing the spread of infection also helps stays within healthcare capacity.

COVID-19 and help flatten the curve. This can reduce the risk of our healthcare system becoming overwhelmed and, quite likely, fewer people will die.

We do not all inevitably get food poisoning, SARS, norovirus, and Ebola. These viral diseases that do not have vaccines are avoided for the most part by behavioral changes. So, it is not the case that we must all now get COVID-19.

**READ MORE**

**[U1.7]**  Site where you can find the COVID-19 status for where you are and other geographical locations
[https://healthblog.uofmhealth.org/wellness-prevention/flattening -curve-for-covid-19-what-does-it -mean-and-how-can-you-help]

**[U1.8]**  Article with interactive infection spread simulations
[https://www.washingtonpost.com/graphics/2020/world/corona-simulator/]

# Quiz 1: Flattening the Curve

Here is a short quiz about flattening the curve. There are many quizzes throughout the book. Please think about each question and mark your answer with a pen or pencil before turning the page to look at the answer. The questions are another way to get the material to sink in and to practice applying the knowledge. Answering quiz questions is a way of practicing retrieval of declarative information from your memory, which increases the strength of that memory, thus making it easier to turn your declarative knowledge (facts) into procedures (skills). Through practice and proactive behavior, you can help break the chain of infection like the match in Fig. 1.4.

**Fig. 1.4** A row of matches showing how distancing can help stop the spread.

**Question 1.1** Does flattening the curve mean fewer deaths in general?

A) Yes    B) No    C) Maybe

**Question 1.2** Does flattening the curve mean less COVID-19 infections overall?

A) Yes    B) No    C) Maybe

**Question 1.3** Do your personal actions help flatten the curve?

A) Yes    B) No    C) Maybe

**Question 1.4** I am just one person, and I do not have any symptoms, and no one I know does. Will my actions really matter?

A) Yes    B) No    C) Maybe

**Question 1.5** What is the main purpose of helping to flatten the curve?

A) Alert people to when they can stop sheltering in place
B) To give companies time to make more toilet paper and hand sanitizer
C) Reduce the infection rate of senior citizens
D) Increase healthcare capacity
E) Prevent overwhelming the health care system and reduce deaths

### Answers to Quiz 1

#### Question 1.1: C, Maybe
*Feedback:* Maybe. Flattening the curve does not necessarily prevent deaths; it defers deaths in the absence of a vaccine. If a death rate reduction occurs, it will come from two sources where healthcare facilities are not overwhelmed, and thus resources are available:

1. Ventilators and other healthcare resources may now be used in more cases where needed, reducing death.
2. Facilities and resources are available to treat non-COVID-19 cases.

#### Question 1.2: C, Maybe
*Feedback:* Maybe. It depends. With a mild outbreak, flattening the curve can mean less infection, and that the healthcare system will not be overwhelmed. For a particularly dangerous infection, flattening the curve might only mean that the healthcare system is not overwhelmed, which would lead to less suffering and fewer deaths.

#### Question 1.3: A, Yes
*Feedback:* Yes, each person who helps themselves also helps others. The flattening is the addition of everyone who contributes. It requires enough of us. Right now, all of us. We have developed this material to help flatten the curve and save lives. David Quammen, in *Spillover*, notes that individual actions can help stop pandemics in humans, and humans are uniquely able to stop pandemics with their individual actions.

#### Question 1.4: A, Yes
*Feedback:* Yes, because those infected with the coronavirus can infect others possibly days before they feel any effects, if they ever do. That means that someone can spread it to you, and you can spread it to others before you even suspect you are ill.

#### Question 1.5: E, prevent overwhelming the health care system and reduce deaths
*Feedback:* Preventing the healthcare system from being overwhelmed is the main purpose of flattening the curve. Keeping the caseload within the capabilities of the healthcare might also lower the overall death rate and permit vaccine interventions.

# 2

# Theory: An Approach for Stopping Infection

## Theory of Transmission

This section will teach you a theory about how infections are transmitted that you can use to reduce your risk of infection.

Once the virus gets inside your body, it begins to multiply. Your body starts to fight the virus by activating your innate (immediate) and adaptive (delayed) immune systems. The innate and adaptive immune systems response against the virus is what causes the symptoms of the disease. For example, your body temperature will increase (fever) to try to kill the virus, and cells in your lungs will begin to produce more mucus to try to clear away the virus, which causes coughing.

However, symptoms such as coughing or sneezing (Fig. 2.1) are actually beneficial for the virus because, as you cough or sneeze, you expel droplets of mucus that can contain hundreds or thousands of virus particles. As these droplets with viruses in them are spread through the air and fall onto surfaces, they can be inhaled directly or picked up from surfaces by other people, particularly if they land on a high touch surface. The virus can then infect a new person.

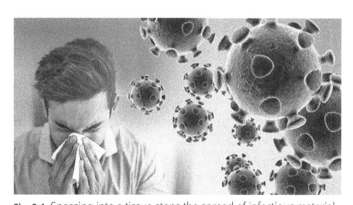

**Fig. 2.1** Sneezing into a tissue stops the spread of infectious material.

Some viruses can be transmitted effectively with very few particles, such as Ebola, whereas other viruses need hundreds or even millions of particles to infect a new person. However, in most cases, there are plenty of virus particles in a single cough or sneeze to transmit most viruses effectively.

**READ MORE**

**[U2.1]**  A useful summary of respiratory disease spread, and how to avoid and mitigate exposure [https://www.erinbromage.com/post/the-risks-know-them-avoid-them]

**[U2.2]**  Search via your favorite search engine: "Experts rate the risks of activities with COVID-19"

**[U2.3]**  A light-hearted demonstration of infection transmission [https://www.cnn.com/videos/entertainment/2020/03/17/scrubs-14-year-old-clip-infection-spread-mxp-vpx.hln]

## Tools to Stop the Spread

The left-hand side of Fig. 2.2 shows the variety of pathways available for infection to spread from one person to the next. The right-hand side shows you skills to help stop the spread. By reducing or eliminating these pathways, you can reduce the likelihood of spreading a virus from an infected individual to a non-infected individual.

Your immune system response is unique to you based on many things such as your age, genetics, current health, environment, and other diseases or medical conditions you may have and have had. Your unique immune system is one of the reasons some people who become infected with a virus may not get very sick, and others infected with the same virus can get very sick or even die. Some people can become infected but never show any symptoms or have very mild symptoms. However, they can still transmit virus particles to other people and can spread the disease. Because of this, we all play an important role in stopping the transmission of the virus, even if we are not visibly sick.

This book teaches you ways to reduce or eliminate these pathways between the person with a virus and an uninfected person. Most of these ways to stop the spread can be done outside your body, which is safer than relying on your adaptive immune system inside your body. When all else has failed, and the infectious agent has gotten into your body, it is the job of the immune system to get rid of the infection.

All of these interventions can be worthwhile even if they are not perfect. For most infections reducing the total number of organisms you are exposed to (viral dose) will decrease the likelihood of becoming infected, so all attempts to minimize exposure are helpful.

Because the COVID-19 virus is so dangerous, especially for seniors and those with chronic conditions, you must treat everyone as if they are infected

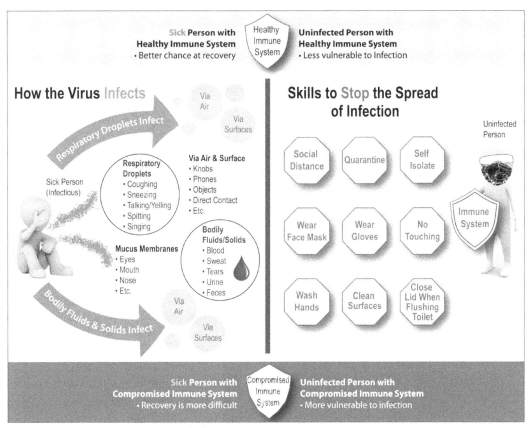

**Fig. 2.2** Tools that help stop the spread of infection.

to protect yourself, and everyone must treat you as if you are infected to protect themselves as well.

Many diseases can still be spread even if the infected person does not appear to be sick. Respiratory viruses like the coronavirus and the flu virus can easily be spread from one person to another from a short distance away through coughing, sneezing, and even breathing. Touching a shared surface with a hand that has touched the nose or mouth or touched a surface where droplets have landed can also spread infections. Some infectious agents require much closer personal contact, such as bodily fluids.

## The Infection Cycle

Because the risk of getting infected seems to be so high, it is extremely helpful to take precautions like assuming everyone (including yourself) is infected. The virus can stealthily sneak into the population when asymptomatic

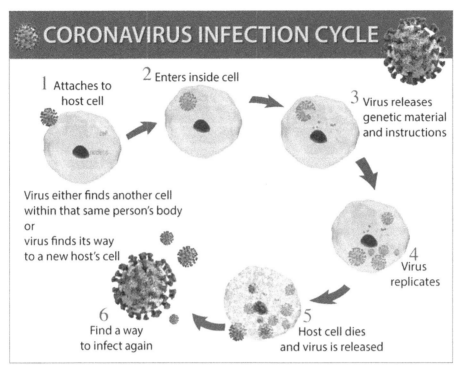

**Fig. 2.3** Diagram of the coronavirus infection cycle.

infected people infect others. Therefore, reducing or stopping the pathways to infection through tools like social (physical) distancing, washing your hands more often, disinfecting surfaces, and avoiding high touch surfaces protects you and those around you.

Fig. 2.3 shows the cycle of infection. A virus wants to complete the cycle so that it can replicate, infect a new host, and repeat. The only way a virus survives is by continuing this cycle. If we treat everyone as infectious, we can outsmart the virus and break the cycle.

**READ MORE**

[U2.4]  Search: "Act like you have coronavirus"

**LEARN MORE**

[U2.5]  A summary of what we know about COVID-19 from the US Department of Homeland Security. Master question list for COVID-19 (caused by SARS-COV-2). Last update, 17 Nov 2020. [https://www.dhs.gov/sites/default/files/publications/mql_sars-cov-2_-_cleared_for_public_release _20201117.pdf]

# Summary of Theory: An Approach for Stopping Infection

Given the theory of infection, anything that blocks the transmission of the infectious materials (the tools on the right side of Fig. 2.2) will help reduce your chance of infection.

**Fig. 2.4** Wearing personal protective equipment is one way to stop the spread. It takes practice to use correctly.

You can reduce infection through any or all of the methods! If you make a mistake, you can remain protected by having multiple defenses. In soccer and cybersecurity, this is called defense in depth.

You want to decrease the possibility of transmission at all stages to protect from the mistakes and oversights that most of us make.

The next section will introduce and help you practice all of these ways to block transmission. Because many of these practices run counter to non-pandemic behavior and habits, you will need to practice (Fig. 2.4).

# Quiz 2: Personal Activities That Can Increase the Risk of Exposure

Here is a quiz about activities that can or cannot increase your risk of exposure. This quiz (also in Appendix 1) will help you judge risk. It is used twice in the book. It is used here as an introduction to the skills, and it is used at the end of the book because it makes a great book summary and discussion activity. Please turn to Appendix 1 and complete the Part 1 quiz for this set of questions about skills to obstruct pandemics. Then, do the rest of this quiz.

**Fig. 2.5** Sneezing or coughing directly on another person can increase the risk of exposure.

**Question 2.1**  If someone is not apparently sick, can their sneeze infect you?

A) Yes    B) No    C) Maybe

**Question 2.2**  If your hands are just washed, can you safely touch your face?

A) Yes    B) No    C) Maybe

**Question 2.3**  Can touching your skin with dirty hands give you an infection?

A) Yes    B) No    C) Maybe

**Question 2.4**  If you feel well, can you infect others, including family members?

A) Yes    B) No    C) Maybe

**Question 2.5**  What is the point of testing my mother in a nursing home when she is not sick?

A) The test directly helps protect her.
B) The test might find out if she is asymptomatic and can thus help reduce transmission.
C) The test helps fund the nursing home.
D) The test is useful to practice for nurses.

## Answers to Quiz 2

**Question 2.1: A, Yes**
Feedback: Yes, for many infections, people can be asymptomatic while still infectious, so sneezes can still carry risks. It varies by disease. The coronavirus is an example of a virus where an individual can be asymptomatic and still be infectious.

**Question 2.2: A, Yes**
Feedback: Yes, after washing your hands is the best time to touch your face! But wash your face, or you can contaminate your hands and possibly your mucous membranes.

**Question 2.3: C, Maybe**
Feedback: Maybe, you can get infected by contaminants on your hands if your skin is cut or broken. Otherwise, the skin does a pretty good job. The chances will vary based on what type of cells the bacteria or virus targets. A respiratory illness like COVID-19 is harder to transmit through a cut in the skin.

**Question 2.4: A, Yes**
Feedback: Yes. With some diseases, you can infect others before you show signs of being sick, or even without ever showing signs of being sick. These diseases tend to spread rapidly.

**Question 2.5: B, the test might find out if she is asymptomatic and can thus help reduce transmission because she can be isolated while she is infectious.**
Feedback:  Testing your mother might help find out if she is asymptomatic and help stop the spread in her nursing home because she can be isolated while she is infectious but not visibly sick.

# 3

# Theory: Infection Theory for Application

## Why You Need a Theory of Infection: Novel Situations and to Help Remember

It would be difficult to illustrate every possible infection risk factor that you may encounter in your day. Everybody has unique day-to-day activities and interacts with different scenarios that may increase their risk of infection.

It is also hard to learn and retain unrelated facts and skills. A theory of why and how to apply procedural skills to new situations can be helpful. With a simple understanding of how infections occur and spread, you can then understand how the interventions we describe can be applied to your specific needs and make the appropriate decisions to reduce your risk.

Fig. 3.1 shows the most common ways that infections can be spread (the rectangles). The virus that causes COVID-19 is a respiratory tract infection and spreads primarily through droplets produced when an infectious person coughs or sneezes. The figure shows that when you inhale infectious droplets released from an infectious person when they sneeze, cough, breathe, or talk, you can get the virus. This route is believed to be the primary route of transmission for SARS-CoV-2.

Fig. 3.1 also shows secondary routes of transmission, such as when you touch a contaminated surface (maybe a countertop that was sneezed on) and touch your face, rub your eyes, or grab a sandwich and eat it. This contact transfers the virus into your eyes, nose, or mouth. According to the CDC, getting the virus from infected surfaces is less common than by inhaling droplets. By avoiding high touch objects, washing your hands, decontaminating surfaces, and trying not to touch your face (the vertical lines), you can further reduce the chance of infection through your skills to obstruct pandemics.

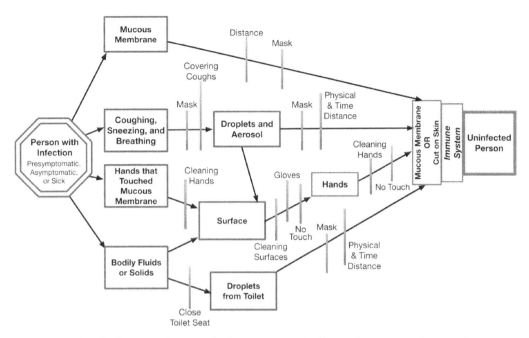

**Fig. 3.1** A model of infection pathways with obstructions (vertical lines) that can stop the spread.

A route of transmission for SARS-CoV-2 not described in Fig. 3.1 is the transmission of the virus from pets to humans and humans to pets. This is because there have been very few cases of pets, such as cats and dogs, that have tested positive for the virus. The CDC notes (9 Sep. 2020) that the risk of getting COVID-19 from pets and transmitting the virus to pets is low. Until more is learned about how this virus affects animals, the CDC recommends treating pets as you would other human family members to protect each other from possible infection. Contact your veterinarian if your pet gets sick, or you have any concerns about your pet's health.

**READ MORE**

[U3.1]  Physical distancing, face masks, and eye protection work, *The Lancet*
[https://www.thelancet.com/pdfs/journals/lancet/PIIS0140-6736(20)31142-9.pdf]

[U3.2]  Coronavirus information specific to pet owners
[https://www.cdc.gov/coronavirus/2019-ncov/daily-life-coping/pets.html]

# Microorganisms Are Everywhere

Microorganisms are organisms that are microscopic or invisible to the naked eye. The term microorganisms include viruses, bacteria, and parasites Though we cannot see these microorganisms, they are present everywhere, including places where humans cannot survive, for example, hydrothermal vents in the oceans that reach a temperature of about 400° C (750° F).

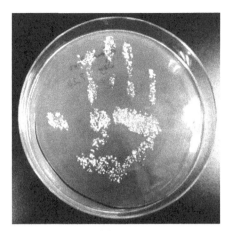

**Fig. 3.2** This petri dish shows bacteria growth from a person's hand that is normally invisible to the naked eye.

Our own body is home to trillions of microorganisms. These microorganisms are mainly present on our skin and our digestive tract. Most are benign or even helpful or necessary, but some microorganisms can be harmful. Fig. 3.2 shows the bacteria that can be grown from a handprint.

## What Are Bacteria?

The word bacterium (singular for bacteria) was derived from the Greek word *baktēria*, which means "staff" or "cane" because of their shape (see Fig. 3.3). Bacteria are single-cell microorganisms that can grow and reproduce independently or act as a parasite and use their host's resources. There are millions of different types of bacteria. Some can be beneficial to their host, and some can cause diseases. Some bacteria are even used in industry to make cheese and antibiotics.

Some bacteria can produce spores. These are like bacteria seeds; they grow into bacteria given the right environment. Spores can last indefinitely.

## What Are Viruses?

What is a Virus? The word virus was derived from the Latin word *virus*, which means "poison" or "slimy liquid." Viruses are microorganisms that are unable to grow or reproduce outside a living cell. Viruses consist of genetic material and proteins that form complex structures and use the host

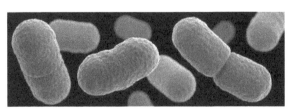

**Fig. 3.3** A computer-generated image of a grouping of *Listeria monocytogenes* bacteria. One cause of food.

cell's resources to replicate itself. They are usually harmful to their hosts.

There are different kinds of viruses. Some viruses have a fatty outer layer. The SARS-CoV-2 virus has that fatty layer, and thus soap and water will easily kill it, as will slightly stronger cleaners.

Coronaviruses are called that because they have a corona or crown around them. Fig. 3.4 shows a model of the SARS-COV-2 virus.

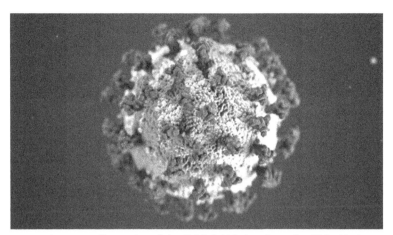

**Fig. 3.4** Computer illustration of the SARS-CoV-2 virus from the CDC with the "crown" or corona shown.

**READ MORE**

**[U3.3]** Article on if viruses are "alive"
[https://www.scientificamerican.com/article/are-viruses-alive-2004/]

## What Are the Differences Between Bacteria and Viruses?

There are several differences between bacteria and viruses. This table helps show what the differences are.

| BACTERIA | VIRUSES |
|---|---|
| Living, reproduces by itself | Requires host cells to reproduce |
| Unicellular (one cell) | Less than a cell |
| Genetic material is DNA | Genetic material is either DNA or RNA |
| Can cause localized or systemic infection | Can cause localized or systemic infection |
| Can be beneficial or harmful to its host | Usually harmful to its host |
| Treated by antibiotics | Treated by antivirals where available, and supporting the patient |
| Vaccines can prevent certain bacterial infections | Vaccines can prevent certain viral infections |
| Can live for seconds to days on surfaces Spores can last indefinitely | Can survive for seconds to days on surfaces |
| Can be killed by heat, UV light, alcohol, cleaners, and antibiotics | Can be destroyed by heat, UV light, alcohol, cleaners |

**Fig. 3.5** Some differences between bacteria and viruses.

# Antibiotics and Bacteria

Many bacterial infections can be treated with antibiotics. Examples include anthrax that can be treated with ciprofloxacin and staph infections that can be treated with penicillin. Many antibiotics can be used to treat a variety of bacterial infections, so you should always consult your doctor to receive the proper antibiotic. Antibiotics can be applied in a cream, injected into a muscle, taken as a pill, or given intravenously (IV). Antibiotics are relatively effective against bacterial infections if they are caught in time. Fig. 3.5 shows such an infection. Antibiotics may also be prescribed when you are ill to avoid secondary infections or when you are fighting another infection already.

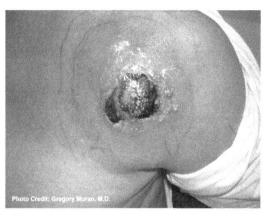

**Fig. 3.5** An abscess caused by the MRSA (Methicillin-resistant *Staphylococcus aureus*) bacteria.

# Antibiotics, Vaccinations, and Viruses

Viral infections **cannot** be treated with antibiotics. They are most commonly prevented by vaccinations (Fig. 3.6). Vaccinations have been produced to prevent you from getting many viral infections, such as the flu, measles, mumps, and rubella. However, these vaccines are very specific for a particular type of virus and do not protect you from other viruses.

There are also antiviral medications available for some viral infections, but like viral vaccinations, these medications are usually specific for a particular virus. These include Tamiflu for influenza and related diseases, and antiretroviral combination drugs for HIV. However, most viral infections do not have direct treatment. The treatment of choice for most viral infections is to simply support the body to fight off the infection.

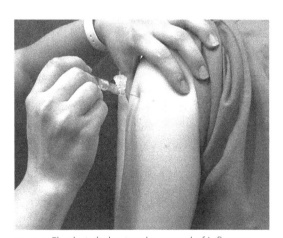

**Fig. 3.6** Flu shots help stop the spread of influenza (flu) and will help reduce the impact of COVID-19 by removing some illness from the population and decreasing the load on the healthcare system.

## A Virus's Life on Surfaces

**Fig. 3.7** It is important to clean (remove dirt) and then sanitize (remove germs).

Another way to fight all infections is to remove them from the environment (Fig. 3.7). The amount of time that the SARS-CoV-2 virus can survive in the air and on surfaces is still being researched. However, studies that have already been done [U3.4, U3.5] show that the coronavirus can survive (be active):

- Up to 3 hours in the air after someone coughs or sneezes
- 4 hours on copper surfaces
- 24 hours on cardboard
- 2-3 days on plastic or stainless steel

These numbers tell you how often you have to clean and what surfaces could be contaminated. These studies were conducted in a laboratory setting, and the time that the virus spends on surfaces can vary in everyday life based on environmental factors. Studies looking at other environmental factors such as humidity, temperature, and UV exposure are still in progress.

**READ MORE**

**[U3.4]**  Van Doremalen, Neeltje, Trenton Bushmaker, Dylan H. Morris, Myndi G. Holbrook, Amandine Gamble, Brandi N. Williamson, Azaibi Tamin et al. 2020. "Aerosol and surface stability of SARS-CoV-2 as compared with SARS-CoV-1." *New England Journal of Medicine* 382 (16): 1564-1567. [https://www.medrxiv.org/content/10.1101/2020.03.09.20033217v1.full.pdf]

**[U3.5]**  SARS lifespan on surfaces calculator [https://www.dhs.gov/science-and-technology/sars-calculator]

## A Virus's Life in the Air

Viruses can also live in the air, and the SARS-CoV-2 virus is not an exception. Typically, the virus is part of a water droplet (Fig. 3.8). Larger sized particles are called droplets, and smaller sized ones are called aerosols, and there are all sizes in-between. Some viruses need a droplet-sized amount to be infectious this way (the flu is an example), and some only need an aerosol (measles is an example). Droplets tend to fall to the ground; aerosols take much longer to drop and thus can travel longer distances. Higher humidity helps the droplets get larger and drop faster.

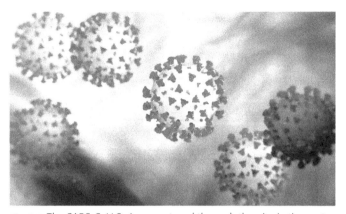

**Fig. 3.8** The SARS-CoV-2 virus can travel through the air via tiny water or mucus droplets when someone sneezes or coughs.

The amount and type of ventilation help define the risk of infection. If you are outside, the air turns over fairly quickly and the volume of air per person is nearly infinite. A breeze also helps disperse particles. There is typically UV light outside during the day, which helps kill (inactivate) the virus, perhaps cutting its lifetime by 10 to 70%, depending on season and time of day. So, being outside, particularly with sunlight, offers some inherent protection from getting infected by virus particles from the air (see U3.6 and U3.8, below).

Where you have a choice, you should prefer to be upwind of a crowd or a potentially infectious person, or ahead of them when walking. Fans can provide this wind for you, particularly on patios.

Similar issues arise with respect to inside air. Super-spreader events (where multiple people are infected) happen much more easily when the air is not turned over with outside air very often, and where the air is not filtered. Hospitals turn over their air very often. Negative pressure rooms pull outside clean air through them, and eject contaminated air through a filter, preventing it from entering other spaces of the building.

Spaces with more equivalent air exchanges are safer than those with less. Closed places without ventilation, by definition, do not turn over nor filter their air. You should be more concerned about wearing personal PPE by you and others where the air is not turned over very often.

Meeting people outside, the use of high-quality air filters for the building or room, turning air over from outside or through filters more often, and opening windows are useful in reducing the spread of COVID-19. Currently, however, we cannot quantify just how much.

### READ MORE

**[U3.6]**  National Academy of Science on UV light and COVID-19
[https://sites.nationalacademies.org/basedonscience/covid-sunscreen/index.htm]

**[U3.7]**  *Wired* article about how to use a fan and filter to clean air
[https://www.wired.com/story/could-a-janky-jury-rigged-air-purifier-help-fight-covid-19/]

**[U3.8]**  SARS lifespan in the air calculator
[https://www.dhs.gov/science-and-technology/sars-airborne-calculator]

# Quiz 3: Viruses, Bacteria, Antibiotics, and Transmission

This quiz asks some questions about bacteria and viruses. Some questions will test your background knowledge. There is no grade, so just do your best.

## Part 1: About pathogens

**Question 3.1**   Are all bacteria harmful?

A) Yes      B) No      C) Maybe

**Question 3.2**   Can both viruses and bacteria cause infections?

A) Yes      B) No      C) Maybe

**Question 3.3**   Do bacteria or a virus cause the common cold?

A) Bacteria      B) Virus      C) Either a virus or bacteria

**Question 3.4**   Do bacteria or a virus cause pneumonia?

A) Bacteria      B) Virus      C) Either a virus or bacteria

**Question 3.5**   Do bacteria require a host cell to reproduce?

A) Yes      B) No      C) Maybe

**Question 3.6**   For each of these conditions, is it caused by a virus or bacteria?

**i) Anthrax?**
A) Bacteria      B) Virus      C) Either a virus or bacteria

**ii) MERS infection?**
A) Bacteria      B) Virus      C) Either a virus or bacteria

**iii) The bubonic plague?**
A) Bacteria      B) Virus      C) Either a virus or bacteria

**iv) The flu?**
A) Bacteria      B) Virus      C) Either a virus or bacteria

**v) Hepatitis?**
A) Bacteria      B) Virus      C) Either a virus or bacteria

**vi) AIDS?**
A) Bacteria      B) Virus      C) Either a virus or bacteria

**vii) Tuberculosis?**
A) Bacteria      B) Virus      C) Either a virus or bacteria

**viii) COVID-19?**

A) Bacteria      B) Virus      C) Either a virus or bacteria

**Question 3.7**    Can cold temperatures in your fridge or freezer kill viruses?

A) Yes      B) No      C) Maybe

**Question 3.8**    Should you use antibiotics for simple viral infections?

A) Yes      B) No      C) Maybe

## Part 2: Objects and events that may transmit an infection

Now that you have read about infection theory, these questions ask you to identify objects, surfaces, and situations that may be able to transmit infections. This understanding is the first step to protecting yourself.

**Question 3.9**    Can you get sick from an uncovered cough or sneeze?

A) Yes      B) No      C) Maybe

**Question 3.10**    Which are the two most important times to wear gloves during the pandemic as recommended by the CDC?

A) When using an ATM at the bank.
B) When caring for a sick individual.
C) When disinfecting surfaces.
D) When going for a walk with the dog.

**Question 3.11**    Can you get sick from using the same bathroom as an infected person?

A) Yes      B) No      C) Maybe

**Question 3.12**    Who should wear masks to protect from COVID-19 spreading in public areas?

A) The sick      B) The well      C) Both

**Question 3.13**    How can you tell if you are asymptomatic?

A) A test for the virus.
B) You can "just feel it."
C) Visible symptoms.

**Question 3.14**    Can you get COVID-19 from touching someone's hands?

A) Yes      B) No      C) Maybe

**Question 3.15** Is a shopping cart handle thoroughly cleaned with disinfectant wipes at the supermarket free from the virus?

A) Yes    B) No    C) Maybe

**Question 3.16a** Which of these conditions reduce the transmissibility of the SARS-CoV-2 virus? (Yes/No)

A) Longer time between you and someone else in the same space
B) Relatively higher humidity
C) Relatively cold temperatures
D) Relatively High temperatures
E) UV light
F) People you like really well
G) Bright gymnasium lights

**Question 3.16b** Which of these conditions reduce the transmissibility of the SARS-CoV-2 virus? (Yes/No)

A) Candlelight
B) Sunlight (it includes UV light)
C) More air exchanges with the outside air
D) Closed rooms
E) HEPA air filters
F) Higher ceilings
G) Mask wearing

. . . . . . . . . . . . . . . . . . . . . . . . . . . . . . . . . . . . . . . . . . . . . . . . . . . . . .

## Answers to Quiz 3

### Part 1: About pathogens

**Question 3.1: B, No**
*Feedback:* No, not all bacteria are harmful. In fact, some bacteria can be beneficial. For example, they help digest food in your intestines and can protect your skin from other bacteria. Some are used in making cheese.

**Question 3.2: A, Yes**
*Feedback:* Yes, both can cause infections, but bacterial and viral infections will generally have different symptoms and treatments depending on the source of the infection.

**Question 3.3: B, Virus**
*Feedback:* The common cold is typically caused by an infection from one or several fairly common viruses.

**Question 3.4: C, Either a virus or bacteria**
*Feedback:* C, either a virus or bacteria. Pneumonia is when your lungs are inflamed. Both bacterial and viral infections can cause this, as can other things, like smoke.

**Question 3.5: B, No**
*Feedback:* No, bacteria do not require a host to survive and can reproduce without a host.

**Question 3.6: i) A, ii) B, iii) A, iv) B, v) C, vi) B, vii) A, viii) B**
*Feedback:*
> i) Anthrax – A, bacteria causes anthrax.
> ii) MERS Infection – B, a virus causes MERS (Middle East Respiratory Syndrome).
> iii) The bubonic plague – A, bacteria causes the bubonic plague.
> iv) The flu – B, a virus causes the seasonal flu.
> v) Hepatitis – C, hepatitis is inflammation of the liver. Typically, hepatitis is caused by viruses, but there can be other causes, including bacteria.
> vi) AIDS – B, AIDS (Acquired Immunodeficiency Syndrome) is caused by HIV (Human Immunodeficiency Virus).
> vii) Tuberculosis – A, bacteria causes tuberculosis.
> viii) COVID-19 – B, the SARS-CoV-2 virus causes COVID-19.

**Question 3.7: B, No**
*Feedback:* No, at such temperatures, like winter weather temperatures, many viruses have an outer covering (also called an envelope), that just hardens to a rubbery gel that shields the virus as it passes from person to person.

**READ MORE**

[U3.9]  Why does flu come during cold weather?
[https://www.nih.gov/news-events/news-releases/nih-scientists-offer-explanation-winter-flu-season]

**Question 3.8: B, No**
*Feedback:* No (but always follow your healthcare provider's medical advice). Generally, antibiotics are not effective against viral infections. However, your healthcare provider may prescribe

an antibiotic to prevent a secondary bacterial infection to protect you while you are sick with a virus. Researchers are currently testing a variety of drugs, including antibiotics, against COVID-19 in an attempt to control the symptoms of this new virus.

## Part 2: Objects and events that may transmit an infection

### Question 3.9: A, Yes
*Feedback:* Yes, you can. So, cover your cough and ask or help others to do so as well.

### Question 3.10: B and C, when caring for a sick individual and when disinfecting surfaces
*Feedback:* Both B and C are the most important times to wear gloves. The CDC recommends wearing gloves when you are cleaning or caring for someone who is sick. Always remember to wash your hands after removing your gloves. When using an ATM, you can easily use sanitizer. If you have a cut on your hand, you should consider wearing gloves when using an ATM.

### Question 3.11: A, Yes
*Feedback:* Yes, you can become infected when someone else has used the bathroom, but there are steps you can take to protect yourself. Make sure the toilet lid is closed before they flush, clean and disinfect surfaces they touched, physically distance yourself, and increase the time between when you use the bathroom after someone who is sick or asymptomatic uses the bathroom. Always close the toilet seat when you flush (in case you are infected but asymptomatic), remember to wash your hands thoroughly, do not touch your face until you have washed your hands, and use a towel to open the door.

### Question 3.12: C, Both the sick and the well
*Feedback:* C, both should wear masks. Masks on the sick will help reduce the viruses they spread (but may not stop it). Masks on the well will reduce the uptake of viruses, although it may not entirely prevent it. Also, it is important to note: masks on the well can help stop the spread if "the well" is someone who is sick but showing no outward symptoms.

### Question 3.13: A, A test for the virus
*Feedback:* A, you can only tell if you are asymptotic with a test. You should treat yourself and others as potentially sick and keep safe through interventions like wearing a mask, washing your hands often, and staying distanced physically.

### Question 3.14: A, Yes
*Feedback:* Yes, you can get the virus on your hands from casual contact (shaking hands or touching what someone else touched) and then touching the mucous membranes on your face (you are not getting infected through the skin of your hand). More importantly, you are close enough to get infected by their coughs or sneezes. So, use interventions like not touching others, maintaining social distance, and cleaning surfaces and objects that may have the potential to be contaminated.

**READ MORE**

[U3.10] Search: "How long does coronavirus live on surfaces?"

### Question 3.15: A, Yes
*Feedback:* Yes, the shopping cart handle after cleaning is as safe as you are going to get! Properly cleaning and disinfecting the shopping cart handle should make it safe to touch.

**Question 3.16a: A, Yes; B, Yes; C, No; D, Yes; E, Yes; F, No; G, No**

*Feedback:* Increasing time, humidity, and temperature all help reduce the transmissibility of SARS-CoV-2. UV lights also help by decontaminating the areas that are lit by UV light. Regular lights that we commonly see do not provide sufficient UV light to decontaminate. Unsurprisingly, whether you know the people or not, the transmissibility remains the same.

**Question 3.16b: A, No; B, Yes; C, Yes; D, No; E, Yes; F, Yes; G, Yes**

*Feedback:* UV light comes from sunlight and can help reduce transmissibility. However, light from candles does not work the same way. Another key to reducing transmissibility is to have greater air movement throughout the area so that the virus can spend less time around other people while it naturally degrades in the air. Minimizing exposure to lingering air droplets from others by having more space and wearing a mask also will help.

# 4

# Theory: The Immune System for Application

## Your Immune System

Your immune system, shown in Fig. 4.1, is a very complex system that protects you against invading organisms like bacteria and viruses that could otherwise make you sick. The immune system consists of the innate and adaptive immune system.

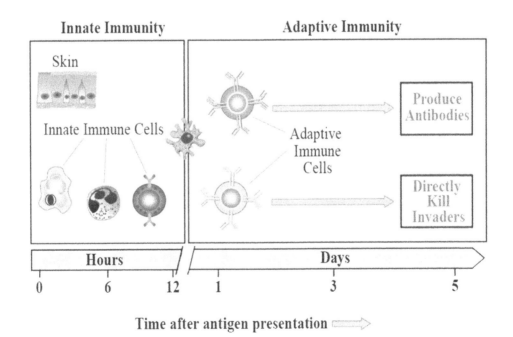

**Fig. 4.1** The innate (left) and adaptive (right) components of the immune response and the respective time course of both.

## Your Innate (Immediate) Immune System

The innate immune system is our first line of defense, and either passively stops or responds immediately to anything it sees as an invader. The innate immune system includes physical barriers such as your skin and tears (Fig.

4.2) that prevent harmful agents from entering your body. The skin especially acts as an effective barrier between pathogens and the body. However, if a virus or bacteria gets through the skin, the body has several other ways to fight it off, including cells of the innate immune system. The innate immune system cells respond immediately to an

**Fig. 4.2** Two major components of the innate immune system are your skin and tears.

invader, but the response is limited and non-specific. The response is called non-specific because it cannot tell the difference between similar pathogens and responds to them the same way. Though non-specific, the innate immune response can stop the virus from spreading throughout your body, and can also help activate the adaptive immune system.

## Your Adaptive (Delayed) Immune System

The adaptive immune system (shown as a dashed line in Fig. 4.3), unlike the innate immune system (shown in dotted line in the figure, with the skin's physical barrier as an bar), takes several days to weeks to mount an effective response to an invader. This delay is mainly because the adaptive immune system tailors its response to that particular pathogen. This extra time makes the adaptive immune system's response more effective than the non-specific response of the innate immune system.

The adaptive immune system cells clear infections by producing antibodies against the invader or by directly killing the invader. The adaptive immune system is also able to "remember" a pathogen it has seen before. This memory allows the adaptive immune system to act quickly if the pathogen tries to infect us again, protecting us from a second infection. Vaccines provide the adaptive immune system with this "memory" of a pathogen without exposing you to the unmodified pathogen.

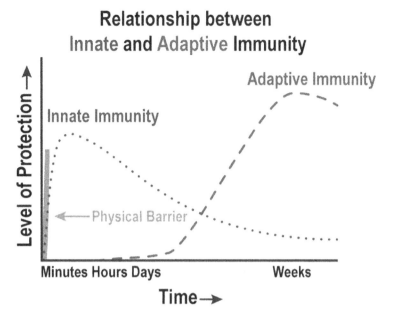

**Fig. 4.3** The response timeframes and level of protection for the innate (immediate) and adaptive (delayed) immune systems.

## Where and How You Shed Infection

As we previously mentioned, viruses need a host, and the host's resources including nutrients to survive and reproduce (make copies of itself). However, the host's resources are not unlimited, and the host's immune system is actively trying to get rid of the virus. So, to survive, the virus must infect other people, and to do this, viruses have developed a strategy called viral shedding.

Viral shedding is the process by which a virus-infected person excretes newly made copies of the virus out of the body to survive by spreading.

There are different routes the virus can use:

- Fecal route—Bowel movements are an activity we all do, and it is our body's way of getting rid of food waste. Viruses take advantage of this normal process and use it to release themself out of the body by being part of your feces or poop.

- Bodily fluids—Bodily fluids include blood, saliva, tears, breast milk, urine, semen, and vaginal fluids. The virus can be present in these fluids and is released into the environment if these fluids are expelled from the body. This is the most common infection route for HIV, for example.

- Respiratory route—The virus can be present in the mucus, saliva, and other parts of the respiratory system. Actions like sneezing, coughing, singing, and talking can release the virus into the environment. This route is probably the most common infection pathway for SARS-CoV-2.

## When You Shed Infectious Material

The time from when an infected person starts to shed a virus and how long it lasts depends on the virus. A person can shed virus before symptoms show up, during the time they have symptoms, and also even after they have recovered. Asymptomatic individuals, who have the virus but show no symptoms, can also shed the virus. Asymptomatic individuals pose a significant problem in controlling the spread of a virus because they and others are unaware that they are shedding the virus.

People with COVID-19 appear to have an unusually wide range of responses to infection. Some, maybe many or even most people, show little or no symptoms. Others may develop symptoms that range from mild to critically ill. A number of these people can spread the infection while not appearing to be sick, or before they become visibly sick (presymptomatic). For a minority of people, when they get infected, they get quite ill, and many of them die. It is currently hard to predict who will end up in each category, but being elderly or having pre-existing medical conditions seem to be strongly associated with severe disease.

The SARS-CoV-2 virus, which causes COVID-19, is thought to use multiple routes for viral shedding. According to the WHO-China Joint Mission on Coronavirus Disease 2019 report, the virus's genetic material was found in feces, respiratory samples, and blood, suggesting the virus is shed through respiratory routes, fecal routes, and through bodily fluids as well. However, further tests need to be done to confirm whether or not the virus in these samples is capable of infecting others.

According to the report, people with moderate disease seem to shed the virus through the respiratory route 1-2 days before the onset of symptoms and continue to shed the virus for up to 7-12 days. In severe cases, the viral shedding through the respiratory route persists up to 2 weeks from the onset of symptoms. The respiratory route appears to be the most prevalent route for COVID-19. Viral shedding may also occur through bowel movements (fecal) for up to five weeks, but shedding is primarily through the respiratory route [U4.1]. More studies need to be done to understand transmission through fecal, blood, and other contact routes.

Asymptomatic carriers shedding the virus are part of the reason it has been hard to control the rapid spread of the virus worldwide, and this is why people are being asked to use precautions as if they have the virus without symptoms.

**READ MORE**

**[U4.1]** Wölfel, Roman, Victor M. Corman, Wolfgang Guggemos, Michael Seilmaier, Sabine Zange, Marcel A. Müller, Daniela Niemeyer et al. 2020. "Virological assessment of hospitalized patients with COVID-2019." *Nature* 581 (7809): 465-469.
[https://doi.org/10.1038/s41586-020-2196-x].

**[U4.2]** Watch a sneeze in slow motion
[https://www.npr.org/sections/health-shots/2016/08/24/490670499/watch-a-slow-motion-sneeze-looks-a-lot-like-breathing-fire]

## Complex Reasons for Masks and Distancing

Figure 4.4 shows what happens in your body when you "catch" COVID-19. Understanding the course of infection curve will help you understand how to stop its spread. After the initial exposure [A], the virus multiplies in your body. The amount of virus in your body is called viral load.

At some point the viral load will become high enough that it can be detected by a test [C]. This level varies by the test, where the test is applied (blood, nose, spit), and somewhat on how the infection is distributed in your body. There may be a time where you are infectious before it can be detected [B], and you can become infectious quickly after a test [B but not yet C], and there may be a time when you are not showing symptoms but are

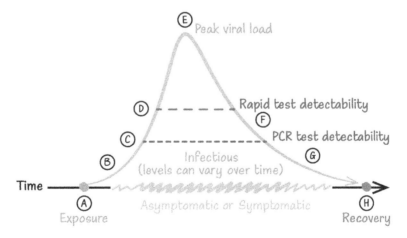

**Fig. 4.4** What happens in your body when you "catch" COVID-19. This graph shows the complexity and dynamic nature of the variables of time, viral load, and testing sensitivity/detectability of the coronavirus. The combination of these variables make it difficult to get a definitive test result. (Note: time and viral load not to scale.)

very infectious [B to G, depending on you], and you can be infectious after being tested and before getting your results. Your viral load may go up, but you might not show symptoms or very strong symptoms [E], which is good for you, but you could still be very infectious depending on your behavior. Masks and distance help reduce how infectious you are.

As the infection goes down [F and then G] the virus is less detectable. There is also a time after you no longer have a testable amount [F or G, depending on the test], but may still be able to shed a little virus. A little virus here, a little virus there, and it is possible for someone to get enough viral dose to become sick themselves. Having a negative test twice moves you further down [G] and are unlikely to still be infectious.

An example of what this could mean for you: You went to a football game on the first of the month [A] and there was someone there who was infectious and who was wearing their mask incorrectly and not social distancing. You also know you plan to visit your grandparents in a week, so you want to be careful and you schedule a PCR test five days after that exposure (still within B on the graph). That test result is negative, so you feel that you are safe to visit your grandparents (at point E). A few days after you visit your grandparents you hear that people from the football game are getting sick, so you decide to get a rapid test just to make sure that you did not expose your grandparents. You take your second test after your viral load has fallen below the point that a rapid test can detect (region F), so the test is negative again. Now, you have never had symptoms and have had two negative test results and feel confident that you were never sick. But you were around your grandparents during your peak viral load, and they may have been exposed.

With this in mind, you can see there is never a time that you can know for sure you are not infectious—unless you have been fully isolated or wear a mask and socially distance all the time. However, you can know that you are infectious after a positive test until sometime after not having another positive test., or approximately when you have a negative test.

**Bottom line:** you should wear a mask to protect others and help others to protect you. The rest of the book teaches you skills to avoid sharing and to avoid catching the disease during these periods.

### READ MORE

**[U4.3]**  Example story of false negatives in testing
[https://www.gq.com/story/julia-ioffe-false-negative-covid-testing]

**[U4.4]**  Article on COVID-19 testing and public health
[https://www.nejm.org/doi/full/10.1056/NEJMp2025631]

# Quiz 4: The Immune System and Shedding Viruses

Now you can test your knowledge about the immune system that will help you prepare to protect yourself and others.

Part 1: The Immune System

**Question 4.1**    Does your skin protect you from viruses?

A) Yes     B) No     C) Maybe

**Question 4.2**    Does the Innate immune system include physical barriers like the skin?

A) Yes     B) No     C) Maybe

**Question 4.3**    Does your skin protect you if it has a cut?

A) Yes     B) No     C) Maybe

**Question 4.4**    MERS-CoV and SARS-CoV-2 (the virus that causes COVID-19) are both coronaviruses. Can our INNATE immune system differentiate between them?

A) Yes     B) No     C) Maybe

**Question 4.5**    SARS-CoV and SARS-CoV-2 (the virus that causes COVID-19) are both coronaviruses. Can our ADAPTIVE immune system differentiate between them?

A) Yes     B) No     C) Maybe

**Question 4.6**    Does the adaptive immune system have the ability to target a specific virus (specificity) and memory?

A) Yes     B) No     C) Maybe

**Question 4.7**    Sayantoni had a full-blown measles infection when she was a child. Now, Sayantoni's daughter has measles. Is Sayantoni at as great a risk of getting measles as her daughter?

A) Yes     B) No     C) Maybe

**Question 4.8**    Does the innate immune system have the ability to target individual bacteria and viruses (specificity and memory)?

A) Yes     B) No     C) Maybe

**Question 4.9** What are the key characteristics of the adaptive immune system that makes it more effective against invaders than the innate immune system?

A) The adaptive immune system has a greater number of cells at its disposal than the innate immune system.
B) The adaptive immune system can act immediately while the innate immune system takes days to respond.
C) The adaptive immune system's response to an invader is specific to that invader, while the innate immune system's response is not. The adaptive immune system also has a memory, unlike the innate immune system.
D) The adaptive immune system can kill cells infected with the invader while the innate immune system cannot.

**Question 4.10** Many viral diseases, including COVID-19, list fever as a symptom. Does the virus or the immune system cause fever?

A) Virus    B) Immune system

**Question 4.11** Can cleaning your hands with sanitizer tell you if you have a cut?

A) Yes    B) No    C) Maybe

## Part 2: Shedding viruses and infecting others

You are about to take a quiz that will help you understand how an individual sheds a virus and infects others.

**Question 4.12** Can you infect someone before you are VISIBLY sick?

A) Yes    B) No    C) Maybe

**Question 4.13** Can you infect someone before you FEEL sick?

A) Yes    B) No    C) Maybe

**Question 4.14** How soon after exposure to the coronavirus can a person infect someone else by SPREADING the virus?

A) Immediately
B) 1 hour
C) 3 days
D) 14 days
E) 1 month

**Question 4.15** How soon after exposure to the coronavirus can a person infect someone else by SHEDDING virus?

A) Immediately
B) 1 hour
C) 3 days
D) 14 days
E) 1 month

**Question 4.16**   Raphael tests positive for COVID-19. The only people he met in the last 14 days were his friends Jill and Sam. Both Jill and Sam also test positive for COVID-19, but Jill is asymptomatic. Which of Raphael's friends gave him the virus?

A) Jill
B) Sam
C) Either of them
D) Neither of them

**Question 4.17**   Mireia had COVID-19 and recently got discharged from the hospital after recovering. What is the longest she could typically continue to shed the virus from the time when her symptoms began?

A) She has recovered and, therefore, is no longer shedding virus
B) 2 days
C) 2 weeks
D) 5 weeks

**Question 4.18**   Can proper handwashing help stop the spread of a virus that is shed through the fecal route?

A) Yes      B) No      C) Maybe

**Question 4.19**   A new virus from a bat infects a human. This virus can infect and reproduce in the human, but the virus is unable to shed from the human. Will the virus survive in the long term?

A) Yes      B) No      C) Maybe

**Question 4.20**   Ari has COVID-19, and he practices good habits like handwashing and staying home when sick. He has recovered and has not infected anyone else. Does this mean that he did not shed the virus?

A) Yes      B) No      C) Maybe

**Question 4.21**   Could you be infectious when . . . ? Yes, no, unlikely.

A) You have not left your house in two weeks
B) You have left your house a week ago to go grocery shopping and had a nice chat with your neighbor at the store
C) You went to an outdoor concert
D) You went to a dinner party outside
E) You got a negative test back

## Answers to Quiz 4

### Part 1: The Immune System

**Question 4.1: A, Yes**
*Feedback:* Yes, the skin is your largest organ and the initial defense against infections, but remember it does not mean you cannot get the virus on your skin, that is why it is important to wash with soap and water, so you do not transfer the virus to a place where it can infect you.

**Question 4.2: A, Yes**
*Feedback:* Yes, physical barriers like your skin are the first line of defense, which is part of your innate immune system.

**Question 4.3: B, No**
*Feedback:* No, the skin cannot protect you in the location where you have the cut. Protect it with a glove or bandage.

**Question 4.4: B, No**
*Feedback:* No, the innate system can only recognize specific patterns that are common to viruses and not present in the human body.

**Question 4.5: A, Yes**
*Feedback:* Yes, our adaptive immune system can recognize variations in viruses in the same family and mounts a specific immune response to each particular virus.

**Question 4.6: A, Yes**
*Feedback:* Yes, it can target a specific virus (specificity or memory). It is the part of the immune system that learns about attackers and then remembers through making and circulating antibodies.

**Question 4.7: B, No**
*Feedback:* No, Sayantoni's adaptive immune system has a memory of the measles virus from the first infection. So, while her immunity does decay with time, this time, the immune system is likely to be more ready and can clear the virus before it causes disease. The measles vaccine does the same thing in a similar manner but more safely and protects us against measles.

**Question 4.8: B, No**
*Feedback:* No, even though the innate immune system response acts immediately, it is limited and non-specific, and so our bodies have also developed the adaptive immune response, which remembers and can target a wider variety of invaders.

**Question 4.9: C, See question text for full answer.**
*Feedback:* C, the adaptive system can mount a very specific response.

**Question 4.10: B, Immune System**
*Feedback:* B, fever is caused by the immune system. Viruses and bacteria like to reproduce at a particular temperature, so the immune system increases the body temperature to make it difficult for them to reproduce.

**Question 4.11: B, No**
*Feedback:* No, but it can be suggestive. Micro-abrasions on the skin can cause a break in the protective barrier of the skin and allow viruses in. These abrasions may or may not feel sensitive

when using hand sanitizers. Also, some people with naturally sensitive skin may be sensitive to some sanitizing substances without there being breaks in the skin.

## Part 2: Shedding viruses and infecting others

**Question 4.12: A, Yes**
*Feedback:* Yes, and it is possible to be infectious without ever being visibly sick. This is called being asymptomatic.

**Question 4.13: A, Yes**
*Feedback:* Yes, if you are asymptomatic, you can infect people while not feeling sick.

**Question 4.14: A, Immediately**
*Feedback:* A, immediately. If you touch a contaminated surface with your hand, you can spread that contamination immediately by touching another person's hand or leaving the contamination on a surface.

**Question 4.15: C, 3 days**
*Feedback:* C, about 3 days. It takes about 3 days after you have been exposed to shed a virus. You can shed a virus, but if you and others practice good health habits such as handwashing and social distancing, you both can prevent the transmission of the virus to other people.

**Question 4.16: C, Either of them**
*Feedback:* C, either Jill or Sam could be the source. Jill and Sam are both positive for COVID-19, and even though Jill is asymptomatic, both can shed the virus and infect others.

**Question 4.17: D, 5 Weeks**
*Feedback:* D, the virus could continue to shed up to 12 days by the respiratory route, and up to five weeks through the fecal route. So, make sure to wash your hands after you use the bathroom and close your toilet seat!

**Question 4.18: A, Yes**
*Feedback:* Yes, washing your hands after going to the bathroom helps remove anything you got on your hands.

**Question 4.19: B, No**
*Feedback:* No, viral shedding is necessary for transmission, and if the virus cannot infect further hosts, it will die off.

**Question 4.20: B, No**
*Feedback:* No. You can shed a virus, but if you practice good health habits such as handwashing and social distancing when sick, you can help prevent the transmission of what virus you shed to other people.

**Question 4.21:**
**A, Unlikely.** You have not left your house in two weeks; you are unlikely to be infectious.

**B, Yes.** You have left your house a week ago to go grocery shopping and had a nice chat with your neighbor at the store. You could be infectious, although unlikely if you were both masked and socially distanced. If you have an immunocompromised house member, you might still wish to wear a mask.

**C, Yes.** You went to an outdoor concert, you could be infectious, and if you have an immuno-compromised house member, you might still wish to wear a mask.  This is a known way to get infected.

**D, Yes.** You went to a dinner party outside, you could be infectious, and if you have an immuno-compromised house member, you might still wish to wear a mask.  This is a known way to get infected.

**E, Unlikely, but possible.** You got a negative test back. It depends on when your test was taken and if you were infectious and if your levels of viral load were detectable to the kind of test you took.

# 5

# Theory: Herd Immunity

## What Is Herd Immunity?

Herd immunity (or community immunity) is a natural phenomenon that, over time, reduces the spread of an infectious disease throughout a community.

Why cover herd immunity? It is not a skill, but it is often in the news and has lessons on how and when to apply good behavior. It is a way that many infections are avoided. Because herd immunity will not save us for a long while, it is still up to you to protect yourself, and by doing so, protect people who live with you and near you.

When someone is infected with a virus like COVID-19, they can spread that virus to other people through close contact as long as the people closest to the infected are susceptible to the virus. However, as more people in the community become immune to the virus, they are no longer susceptible to the virus, and even if they are close to an infected individual, they cannot catch and transmit the virus. This immunity helps break the chain of infection from one person to another. As Fig. 5.1 shows, being in a crowd of people who cannot get sick helps you too.

Community spread is a related concept. If there are only a few infected people, and we can find them, we can track whom they may have infected and quarantine them to stop further spreading. When many people are infected, and they do not appear to be sick, then the infection can spread more easily and it is harder to know who should quarantine. When there are enough infectious people that cannot be tracked, the disease is said to be "community-acquired" or "community spread." When the infection becomes community spread, it is harder to fight.

Herd immunity happens primarily in two ways, either through (a) vaccination or (b) following recovery from the disease itself. Additionally, some people can be relatively immune without being infected. Or herd immunity may be achieved through a combination of these. Scientists do not know yet if those people who recover from COVID-19 will be immune to the virus or how long such immunity may last, but comparing COVID-19 to other similar viruses suggests immunity may last on average for up to 2 years.

Fig. 5.1 also shows that a reduction in disease transmission results from increased immunization. The more infectious a virus is, the higher percentage of immune people are needed to generate herd immunity to stop the spread. Reducing the transmission of an infection, either through immunity

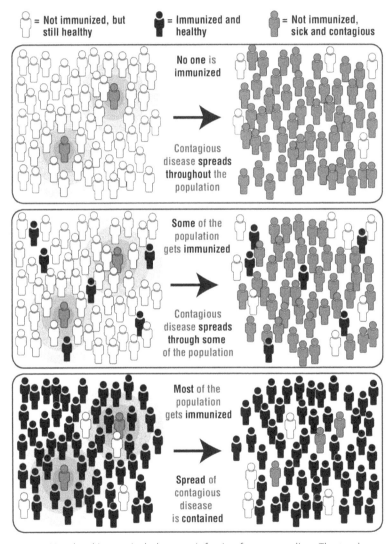

**Fig. 5.1** How herd immunity helps stop infection from spreading. The top box depicts a community in which no one is immunized, and an outbreak occurs. In the middle box, some of the population is immunized but not enough to confer full community immunity. In the bottom box, a critical portion of the population is immunized, protecting most community members.

or by other measures (such as social distancing, masks, and staying home while sick), helps the whole community.

The number of people needed to be immune to provide herd immunity varies based on factors including how easily it spreads, natural immunity, and mitigation measures. We do not yet know the proportion for COVID-19.

## Why Do We Not Have Herd Immunity to COVID-19?

COVID-19 is rapidly spreading because it is a new virus that humans have not been exposed to before. At this point, few people are immune to the virus, although people vary in how susceptible they are to catch it based on their immune system and other risk factors, including age, other illness, and genetic factors. Most people can become infected, and many but not all get sick. There is no current vaccine against the virus, although researchers are working hard to develop a vaccine.

This situation means that most people who are exposed to the virus can become sick or be asymptomatic and still shed enough of the virus to infect others. Herd immunity will not be able to protect the vulnerable members of the community until probably a majority (we do not know the percentage at this point) of people are immune through infection or vaccination. Creating this immunity through infections could overload the healthcare system and cause thousands of deaths.

Because there is currently only partial herd immunity against this disease, there are skills that can obstruct the pandemic by breaking the chain of transmission. These include:

a. Increase the space between sick people (visibly or asymptomatically) who are spreading the virus and healthy people who can catch it. Staying at least 6 feet away from others, "social distancing," will prevent those shedding virus from infecting others.

b. Decrease the amount of virus that infected people can share with others. Infectious droplets are released when an infected person coughs, sneezes, or spits. Aerosols are released when an infected person sings, breaths, coughs, or sneezes. Wearing masks and other protection can stop you from spreading if you are sick (visibly or invisibly) and can help you not get a virus on yourself or breathe it in. Also, coughing and sneezing can be done in ways that spread fewer virus particles.

c. Decrease the possibility of transmission by washing hands, objects, and surfaces. These droplets can also deposit the virus onto surfaces or be transferred when a person coughs or sneezes into their hands and then touches a doorknob, elevator button, money, or anything else the sick person handles (high-touch surfaces).

d. Decrease the transfer of viruses into your body by not touching your mouth, nose, or eyes.

e. Look after your immune system and general health.

These are the "skills to obstruct pandemics" that this book teaches!

## How Are Vaccines Related to Herd Immunity?

Currently, not enough people have been vaccinated or been exposed to the virus to provide herd immunity. As new vaccines are designed, they must be rigorously tested to ensure that they are safe and effective for as many people as possible—you are not exposed to a live pathogen by vaccination. These clinical trials for safety and effectiveness can take 12 to 18 months to perform.

The video in the Learn more link [U5.1] shows how the increasing ratio of vaccinated (yellow) to unvaccinated (blue) individuals in a community slows disease transmission by infected (black) individuals. It does this by decreasing the frequency of interactions between infected and unvaccinated individuals—they just meet less often.

Despite the effort to make vaccines as safe as possible for everyone, there will always be some people who are not able to receive the vaccine or for whom the vaccine is not effective. Very young babies, the elderly, those with other medical complications, or those with allergies to ingredients in the vaccine may not be able to be protected with a vaccine. Therefore, it is important for everyone who is able to receive the vaccine to do so once it is available. Vaccinations help to provide herd immunity and are necessary to protect vulnerable groups who cannot receive the vaccine.

**LEARN MORE**

**[U5.1]** A useful visualization of herd immunity
[https://imgur.com/a/8M7q8]

**[U5.2]** The author's description of the visualization
[https://www.reddit.com/r/dataisbeautiful/comments/5v72fw/how_herd_immunity_works_oc/ddzq37k/]

**[U5.3]** Description of herd immunity from the PBS science documentary series Nova
[http://www.pbs.org/wgbh/nova/body/herd-immunity.html]

**READ MORE**

**[U5.4]** Department of Health Services, Texas presentation on herd immunity
[https://www.dshs.texas.gov/uploadedFiles/Content/Prevention_and_Preparedness/immunize/Measures%20to%20Fight%20Meales%20Outbreaks%20-%20DeBolt%20and%20Fiebelkorn.pdf]

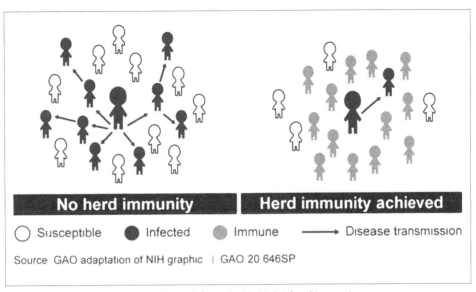

**Fig. 5.2** The spread of disease without (left) and with (right) herd immunity.

## Summary: Herd Immunity

In summary, because we do not have herd immunity (shown another way in Fig. 5.2) or an approved and widely available and used vaccine to COVID-19 as of yet, and because we do not know if and when we will have a vaccine, we need to take more individual and local interventions to help slow the spread.

In the coming sections, we cover these more individual and local skills about how you can directly protect yourself. These skills will also help protect others by making sure that you do not spread COVID-19 if you get it.

## Quiz 5: Why Herd Immunity and Vaccination are Important to Public Health

This quiz will help you understand the idea of vaccinations and the power of herd immunity.

**Question 5.1**   If you have no immunity either naturally or through vaccination, which group are you safer to join?

A) 100 unvaccinated people that can catch a disease
B) 50 vaccinated people that cannot catch a disease and 50 unvaccinated people

**Question 5.2**   Which family is safer to join?

A) A family of 2 people who can catch a disease
B) A family of 2 people who cannot catch a disease

**Question 5.3**   Do vaccines give you the disease they are supposed to protect you from?

A) Yes      B) No      C) Maybe

**Question 5.4**   Are vaccines generally safe?

A) Yes      B) No      C) Maybe

**Answers to Quiz 5**

**Question 5.1: B, 50 vaccinated people that cannot catch a disease and 50 unvaccinated people**
*Feedback:* B, you are safer to join the room with 50 vaccinated people that CANNOT catch a disease and 50 unvaccinated people. The vaccinated people have less of a chance of catching the disease and sharing it with you.

**Question 5.2: B, A family of 2 people who cannot catch a disease**
*Feedback:* B, you are safer with the family who CANNOT catch the disease. If they cannot catch it, they CANNOT share it with you!

**Question 5.3: B, No**
*Feedback:* No, vaccines do not give you the disease. They expose individuals to a very small and very safe amount of pieces of the virus or bacteria that will stimulate your immune system. You may get mild symptoms after a vaccine because your immune system is preparing for the disease as it trains to recognize and attack future exposure to that illness. As a result, you will not become ill, although you may experience mild symptoms. Although a strategy to remain unvaccinated and "hide in the vaccinated-herd" may work briefly, the consequences can be severe, as seen in recent measles outbreaks.

**READ MORE**

**[U5.5]** Article on vaccines by the National Library of Medicine
[https://medlineplus.gov/ency/article/002024.htm]

**Question 5.4: A, Yes**
*Feedback:* Yes, vaccines are considered safe and effective, with benefits that clearly outweigh risks. Each year millions of healthy people, including children, are vaccinated to prevent serious disease and death. Vaccines are developed over several years during clinical trials that test thousands of volunteers. These trials answer important questions about safety, dosage, and reaction prior to public release. There is always a small percentage of people who should not receive the vaccine and a rare amount who may have adverse effects. On balance and on average, vaccines are very well worth it.

**READ MORE**

**[U5.6]** Vaccination usage worldwide by WHO
[https://www.who.int/en/news-room/fact-sheets/detail/immunization-coverage]

**[U5.7]** Vaccine safety by Children's Hospital of Philadelphia
[https://www.chop.edu/centers-programs/vaccine-education-center/vaccine-safety/are-vaccines-safe]

**[U5.8]** Vaccine safety by US Dept. of Health and Human Services
[https://www.vaccines.gov/basics/safety]

# 6

# Social Distancing: Shelter in Place, Quarantine, and Isolation

## Overview of Social Distancing: Spacing and Hand Shaking

Social distancing is the practice of keeping away from another person to reduce the risk of being exposed to a virus they may be carrying and not infecting someone else with a virus you may not know you are carrying. With many respiratory viruses, including COVID-19, the appropriate distance to maintain between people is at least six feet (two meters or one fathom) to ten feet when possible. This distance is based on how far infectious droplets can spread when someone coughs or sneezes or breathes over an extended period of time. A greater distance is typically safer. You might also wish to consider staying at "mark twain," which is two fathoms or 12 feet. This distance is the safe depth for a riverboat, and is where the writer Mark Twain got his name.

Remember that even people who do not look sick may still be shedding the virus, so social distancing should be practiced with everyone!

**Fig. 6.1** Social distancing helps keep people safe and is necessary for people in high-risk categories.

Social distancing is different from quarantining. When social distancing, you can still do many of your typical day to day activities such as going outside, shopping, or working as long as you remember to keep at least six feet of space between you and other people. Six feet can be remembered as approximately the span of an average adult's arms, fingertip to fingertip, or a little more than the average adult height.

Be aware that there are many places that it may not be possible to keep at least 6 feet away from people, such as inside an elevator or on public transportation. You may need to change your daily routine to avoid places where you cannot distance yourself from others.

Also, being outside helps reduce the spread. The airspace is larger, and there are often breezes. Breezes help disperse and dilute the infectious material. If there is a large group, you may wish to be upwind of them. And if you find yourself inside with the ability to open a window, that may be something to try to keep the circulation of air going.

**READ MORE**

[U6.1]  The level of risks for several activities
[https://www.vox.com/2020/5/22/21266756/coronavirus-pandemic-covid-risks-social-distancing-chart]

[U6.2]  Social distancing correlates with lower infection rates
[https://www.thelancet.com/journals/laninf/article/PIIS1473-3099(20)30553-3]

# Examples of Social Distancing

Social distancing suggests maintaining 6 feet of separation. Fig. 6.2 below shows one way to judge six feet. This space can also be seen as a pair of skis, or two shopping carts touching (it is a bit more, but that is okay). You will have a chance to judge this distance in several ways in the quiz.

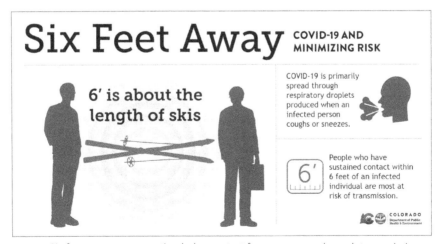

**Fig. 6.2** Six feet or more separation helps protect from sneeze and cough transmission.

**LEARN MORE**

**[U6.3]**  Public service announcement from the State of Ohio illustrating the effect of social distancing [https://www.youtube.com/watch?v=o4PnSYAqQHU]

# Shelter in Place vs. Quarantine vs. Isolation

Quarantine is when you are restricted to an area, perhaps your own house, or a hospital room because you have been exposed. It has been used informally when you should not be exposed because you are high risk. If you are in a high-risk group, you should essentially self-quarantine or shelter in place. If you self-quarantine, your whole household should as well. You are not allowed to leave your quarantine area, nor have anyone come in. This area might include your yard. This approach is a useful way to have numerous preventative measures implemented automatically for you

**Fig. 6.3** If you have been exposed to COVID-19 you should self-quarantine, and if you are sick or have a positive COVID-19 test, you should isolate.

because there are no surfaces that have to be protected and no other people to infect you or be infected. It is like buying those preventative measures in bulk. The downsides are the restrictions; the upside is that you and others are much safer. If you are sick, you should self-isolate, as Fig. 6.3 suggests.

Fig. 6.4 explains three terms to represent how people will stay at home. These are based on the PA Dept. of Health definitions. These terms are often used interchangeably by many people. They all focus on staying at home to limit exposure to other people.

If you cannot stay home, you will want to minimize contact with other people while fulfilling your job and maintaining friendships. Minimizing contact can mean distance, masks, and other barriers and aids, including being outside.

**Fig. 6.4** Sheltering in place, quarantining, and self-isolating are used for different situations to help stop the spread of infection.

**READ MORE**

[U6.4]   New York Times article on why to stay home
[https://www.nytimes.com/2020/04/11/opinion/sunday/coronavirus-hospitals-bronx.html]

[U6.5]   Search "Quarantine"

## Shelter in Place

Shelter in place is less restrictive than quarantine. You are instructed to stay at home and only leave for essential tasks, such as going grocery shopping (go during off-peak hours, and early if you are particularly at risk), or necessary medical appointments (check with your healthcare provider if you are not sure), or picking up medicine. During those trips, you are strongly urged to maintain social distance and wear masks. You can typically walk for your own and your dog's exercise in your neighborhood, but still maintaining

**Fig. 6.5** Staying at home helps reduce the spread and protect health care workers and the system from overload.

social distance. And you can work in your yard. Non-essential businesses, which are most businesses, are closed.

If you are an essential employee, such as a health care worker, or maintain or run infrastructures such as power or water or work in a grocery store, you can travel to work.

The behavior of sheltering in place helps reduce the number of people you can meet and will meet, and this lowers your chance of either contracting the disease or sharing it with others, as noted in Fig. 6.5. That is to say, you want to limit the number of new people you meet. Fig. 6.6 presents a humorous algorithm for sheltering in place.

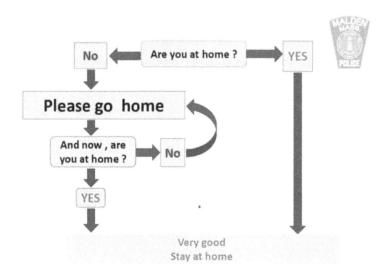

**Fig. 6.6** A humorous flow chart from the Malden (MA) Police explaining how to "shelter in place" and thus reduce the spread of disease.

**READ MORE**

**[U6.6]**  Safety advice if you must visit the grocery store
[https://www.wsj.com/articles/safety-advice-if-you-must-visit-the-grocery-store-11585336520]

# Quiz 6: Social Distancing

This quiz will ask you social distancing questions to help practice your understanding of it. Fig. 6.7 shows another way to measure it.

## Part 1: Social Distancing

**Question 6.1**   When you are maintaining social distance, can you go outside?

A) Yes     B) No

**Question 6.2**   My friend Alice is healthy; therefore, is it safe for me to associate with her closer than 6 feet?

A) Yes     B) No

**Fig. 6.7** Another way to measure six feet.

## Part 2: Measuring appropriate social distance

In this section, you will be asked to judge if the distances are great enough to provide social distancing.

**Question 6.3**   Are the people in this picture maintaining social distance?

A) Yes     B) No

**Question 6.4**   Are the people in this picture maintaining social distance?

A) Yes     B) No

**Question 6.5**    Is going to a party and staying at least six feet apart social distancing?

A) Yes    B) No

**Question 6.6**    For each person, are they at least six feet away from anyone else and maintaining correct social distancing? Find pairs that are and are not safely distanced.

**Person 1 and Person 2?**
A) Yes    B) No

**Person 6 and Person 5?**
A) Yes    B) No

**Person 4 and Person 2?**
A) Yes    B) No

**Person 1 and Person 5?**
A) Yes    B) No

**Person 3 and Person 4?**
A) Yes    B) No

**Person 2 and Person 3?**
A) Yes    B) No

**Question 6.7**    Do two average-sized golden retrievers standing snout to tail provide 6' of social distance?

A) Yes    B) No    C) Maybe

**Question 6.8**    Does one length (laying prone) of the basketball player, Shaquille O'Neil provide 6' of social distance?

A) Yes    B) No    C) Maybe

**Question 6.9**    Does standing across a street provide 6' of social distance?

A) Yes    B) No    C) Maybe

**Question 6.10**    Do two people's spread arms provide 6' of social distance?

A) Yes    B) No    C) Maybe

**Question 6.11**    Does a chair-width apart provide 6' of social distance?

A) Yes    B) No    C) Maybe

**Question 6.12**    Does standing across a single shopping cart provide 6' of social distance?

A) Yes    B) No    C) Maybe

**Question 6.13**    Does standing across a car (either direction) provide 6' of social distance?

A) Yes    B) No    C) Maybe

### Part 3: Sheltering in place, quarantining, and isolation

This quiz will help you understand the differences between sheltering in place, quarantine, and isolation, and how each can help stop the spread of infectious diseases.

**Question 6.14**    You just found out your housemate tested positive for COVID-19. Who should self-isolate, and who should quarantine?

A) Both you and your housemate should quarantine together.
B) Both you and your housemate should self-isolate.
C) Your housemate should quarantine, and you should self-isolate.
D) Your housemate should self-isolate, and you should quarantine.

**Question 6.15**    Does a quarantine protect you from all illness?

A) Yes    B) No    C) Maybe

**Question 6.16**    Does quarantining help flatten the curve?

A) Yes    B) No    C) Maybe

**Question 6.17**    Does sheltering in place help flatten the curve?

A) Yes    B) No    C) Maybe

**Question 6.18**    Does isolation help flatten the curve?

A) Yes    B) No    C) Maybe

**Question 6.19**    Does the isolation of sick people help flatten the curve?

A) Yes    B) No    C) Maybe

**Question 6.20**    When a state has asked for you to shelter in place: if Ian has high school friends over to play video games and they stay 6' apart, is he putting his 70-year-old grandma who lives with him at risk?

A) Yes    B) No    C) Maybe

**Question 6.21**    If you have a fever, is it safe to go outside to shop?

A) Yes      B) No      C) Maybe

**Question 6.22**    If you have a new dry cough, is it safe to have friends into your home?

A) Yes      B) No      C) Maybe

**Question 6.23**    When a state has asked for shelter in place, can you visit your mom because she is lonely?

A) Yes      B) No      C) Maybe

**Answers to Quiz 6**

Part 1: Social Distancing

**Question 6.1: A, Yes**
*Feedback:* Yes, you can go outside while maintaining social distancing, but should be careful to avoid being near others. And, if you have to go through doors or past people, you will have to take precautions. Going outside is generally good for you, and it is easier to keep social distance in most cases.

**Question 6.2: B, No**
*Feedback:* No. Either of you may still carry the virus and might not yet show symptoms (pres-ymptomatic), or not ever show symptoms (asymptomatic), so breaking social distancing still carries risks.

Part 2: Measuring appropriate social distance

**Question 6.3: B, No**
*Feedback:* No, they are too close.

**Question 6.4:  A, Yes**
*Feedback:* Yes, they are at least six feet apart.

**Question 6.5: B, No**
*Feedback:* No, social distancing is about maintaining six feet while doing essential activities. Going to a party is not an essential activity. Social distancing is about keeping a distance from people whom you have limited contact with, such as at a grocery store or passing someone on the street. Having sustained contact with people such as at a party or other gathering increases your risk of exposure to the virus.

**Question 6.6: Person 1 and 2 – B, No. All others – A, Yes.**
*Feedback:* Person 1 and Person 2 are too close, but all others are appropriately distanced.

**Question 6.7: A, Yes**
*Feedback:* Yes, grown golden retrievers usually measure over three feet long from tail to snout.

**SOCIAL DISTANCING**
*Six feet or more helps protect from sneeze and cough transmission*

├— Six feet —┤

*Two average sized golden retrievers*
*✓ are approximately six feet*

**Question 6.8: A, Yes**

*Feedback:* Yes, Shaq is a bit over seven feet tall, so you will have room to spare.

### SOCIAL DISTANCING
*Six feet or more helps protect from sneeze and cough transmission*

*Shaq's stands at a height of seven feet and one inch*
*✓ (13 inches of extra protection)*

**Question 6.9: A, Yes**

*Feedback:* Yes. While it depends to a certain extent on the street, a good rule of thumb is to think that an average car width is between 6 and 6.5 feet. So, if a road can hold a car or more width-wise, then that is a good indicator that it is at least 6 feet. The people in this picture appear to be practicing social distancing.

**Question 6.10: A, Yes**

*Feedback:* Yes, the arm length of the average adult is about 25 inches, which is less than half of 6 feet or 72 inches. But if two people each put up their arms and add a little more space, then it is about right.

**Question 6.11: B, No**

*Feedback:* No. This chair is about 18 inches wide x 18 inches deep x 30 inches to the highest point. It does not provide 6 feet of distance.

**Question 6.12: B, No**

*Feedback:* No, the average shopping cart is 33 inches long, so even with outstretched arms, one is well short of 6 feet. But, add a little extra space on each side, and you can get 6 feet.

**Question 6.13: A, Yes**

*Feedback:* Yes, because most cars are at least 6 feet wide and even longer in both directions.

## Part 3: Sheltering in place, quarantining, and isolation

**Question 6.14: D, your housemate should self-isolate, and you should quarantine.**
*Feedback:* D, because your housemate tested positive, they should self-isolate until they are symptom-free for at least 3 days and at least 10 days since their symptoms started to keep from infecting others (including distancing themselves from you). If they were asymptomatic, they should count their ten days of isolation from the date of their positive test. Because you were in close contact with them, you may have been infected, and quarantining will keep you from infecting others. Usually, if you were infected, any symptoms will appear within two weeks or less, so your self-quarantine should last for 14 days. (Note: The timing of isolating and quarantining is as of 28 November 2020 and may change in the future. Check the WHO's website: https://www.who.int/news-room/commentaries/detail/criteria-for-releasing-covid-19-patients-from-isolation) and the CDC's website.

**Question 6.15: B, No**
*Feedback:* No, but quarantine can protect you from infectious people during a pandemic. Previous infection agents (viruses, bacteria) can be left in your quarantine area unless you clean the area again, but once clean, it is generally safer. If you go out of your quarantine area, you have to take further precautions.

**Question 6.16: A, Yes**
*Feedback:* Yes. People who are quarantining are absolutely not part of the spreading pattern.

**Question 6.17: A, Yes**
*Feedback:* Yes. People who are sheltering in place are absolutely not part of the spreading pattern.

**Question 6.18: A, Yes**
*Feedback:* Yes. People who are infectious and isolate are not going out and are not part of the spreading pattern.

**Question 6.19: A, Yes**
*Feedback:* Yes. The isolated sick are not part of the spreading pattern.

**Question 6.20: A, Yes**
*Feedback:* Yes, non-essential meetings like this put the elderly and other household members at risk because the visitors could be asymptomatic, and this is a risk that is not part of a shelter in place order. Ian should consider online game-playing to interact with his friends.

**Question 6.21: B, No**
*Feedback:* No, if you have a fever you should stay in and call your doctor or a hotline. You could be infectious and could infect other people.

**Question 6.22: B, No**
*Feedback:* No, you should stay in and call your doctor or a hotline if you have a new dry cough.

**Question 6.23: B, No**
*Feedback:* No, non-essential meetings like this put the elderly and other household members at risk because the visitors (you!) could be asymptomatic, and this is a risk that is not part of a shelter in place order. You should consider a phone call or an online video chat. Wearing a mask, keeping social distance, and meeting outdoors would keep the risk down if you do go.

# 7
# Social Distancing: Not Shaking Hands

## Handshaking

This section teaches you why shaking hands is an activity to avoid and how to avoid it by choosing safer alternatives.

Shaking hands is a common way to greet people (Fig. 7.1). It has a long tradition, and most people like to do it when they see friends and family and when they are meeting new people. It is, however, an extremely easy way to spread microscopic material between people.

**Fig. 7.1** Senator Casey (PA) shaking hands at a construction site (pre-pandemic).

"I don't think we should ever shake hands again. . . . [handshaking] is really one of the major ways that you can transmit a respiratory illness" (Anthony Fauci, Director of the National Institute of Allergy and Infectious Diseases). Many hands are dirty, from wiping a nose or touching surfaces. You might have a virus and not know it, and they might too have a virus and not know it. Thus, when you shake hands, it is easy to pass infectious materials between people without knowing it.

It is also the case that when you are close enough to shake hands, you are violating social/physical distance, which may or may not be a restriction you are under as well. If you do shake hands, or you are compelled, you can use hand sanitizer afterward to minimize the risk.

## Alternatives to Shaking Hands

When you are asked to shake hands, you can note that it is safer for the both of you not to shake hands, or note that your doctor recommends that you do not, or that the CDC recommend that you do not at this time.

**Fig. 7.2** Alternatives to shaking hands that can be done from afar.

**When social distancing is NOT required**

There are alternatives to shaking hands. You can say goodbye, you can wave, or you can bow. When you are not under social distancing restrictions, you can also elbow bump or kick shoes.

**When social distancing is required**

When social/physical distancing is required, you can still wave or bow. You should, however, NOT elbow bump or touch feet because these activities will put you within 6' of another person. Examples are shown in Fig. 7.2.

## When Is Social Distancing Not Required

When is social distancing not required? It is not necessary between people within your household who are not sick. If you are outside and traveling together, you can stay close to each other and hold your children's hands.

**Fig. 7.3** Social distancing is not needed within a family that has no pre-existing conditions and has not been exposed to high-risk situations.

Within your house, you may wish not to share as much. For example, you might want to have separate towels, even hand towels; you should not eat with the same utensils and not serve yourself food using your own utensils.

If you have housemates or family particularly at risk and a family member has to travel outside of the house often, you might wish to consider wearing masks when close to each other.

# Quiz 7: When to Shake Hands and How to Greet Others.

**Part 1: When to shake hands.**

This quiz will give you an awareness of the risk one takes when shaking someone's hand. The quiz will reference some images shown below.

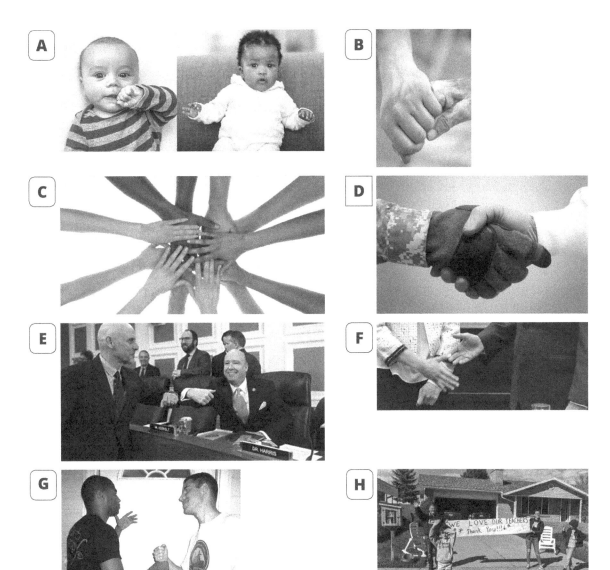

**Question 7.1**   If you met the babies from photo A on the street, is it safe to shake their hand or hug them?

A) Yes      B) No      C) Maybe

**Question 7.2**   Is it safe to hold your grandparent's hand like in photo B?

A) Yes      B) No      C) Maybe

**Question 7.3**   Is it safe to touch these hands in photo C at the end of band camp?

A) Yes      B) No      C) Maybe


**Part 2: How to Greet People When Social Distancing Is Required**

Here are some questions for you to see if you can judge how and when not to shake hands when social/physical distancing is also involved.

**Question 7.4**   Can I hug instead of shaking hands?

A) Yes      B) No      C) Maybe

**Question 7.5**   Does photo D show an appropriate way to shake hands with someone when not social distancing?

A) Yes      B) No      C) Maybe

**Question 7.6**   Can I do a high-five without gloved hands?

A) Yes      B) No      C) Maybe

**Question 7.7**   Does photo E show an appropriate way to greet someone when social distancing?

A) Yes      B) No      C) Maybe

**Question 7.8**   Does photo F show an appropriate way to greet someone when social distancing?

A) Yes      B) No      C) Maybe

**Question 7.9**   Does photo G show an appropriate way to greet someone when social/physical distancing is required?

A) Yes      B) No      C) Maybe

**Question 7.10** Does photo H an appropriate way to greet someone when social distancing?

A) Yes      B) No      C) Maybe

## Answers to Quiz 7

### Part 1: When to shake hands

**Question 7.1: B, No**
*Feedback:* No, while cute, these babies could be excellent little germ monsters.

**Question 7.2: B, No or C, Maybe.**
*Feedback:* No/Maybe are correct answers. If you need to help your older relative, you need to wash your hands before you do it and have them wash their hands afterward, too. It is safer not to do it.

Casual handholding is not safe. If you need to assist an elderly relative, then you and they should wear gloves and a mask if possible. If gloves and a mask cannot be worn, then both sets of hands should be washed or disinfected immediately afterward.

**Question 7.3: B, No**
*Feedback:* No. Because you do not know if any of them are carrying the virus, it is safest not to touch them. If you have to, wash your hands after touching theirs. You do not know, and there is no easy way to find out.

### Part 2: How to greet people when social distancing is required

**Question 7.4: B, No**
*Feedback:* No. You will break the six feet distancing rule, unless you are in personal protective equipment, and even then, not a great idea because you can disturb your equipment unnecessarily.

**Question 7.5: A, Yes**
*Feedback:* Yes, as long as you do not touch your face, and you do not bend your elbows.

**Question 7.6: B, No**
*Feedback:* No, you are still making hand contact. If you should be social distancing, then high-fives still put you within 6 feet of the other person.

**Question 7.7: B, No**
*Feedback:* No, while they are not shaking hands, they are not 6 feet apart.

**Question 7.8: B, No**
*Feedback:* No, they are too close.

**Question 7.9: B, No**
*Feedback:* No, they are too close, and their hands are touching.

**Question 7.10: A, Yes**
*Feedback:* Yes, this is excellent. Note: this is a family that resides in the same household.

# 8

# Social Distancing: Coughing and Sneezing Safely

## How Coughing and Sneezing Work, What They Do

Fig. 8.1 illustrates how, when you cough, you are clearing material, mostly liquids, out of your throat and lungs. This material ends up either in your mouth or coming out of your mouth. What comes out into the air can be classified by its size. Larger particles are called droplets, and smaller particles form an aerosol. There are all sizes in between.

**Fig. 8.1** Droplets dispersing from a sneeze.

In a recent article Bromagh [U8.1], an epidemiologist, suggests the following rule of thumb:

### The Formula for Successful Infection = Exposure-to-Virus x Time

A single cough releases about 3,000 droplets, and droplets travel up to 50 miles per hour. Most droplets are large and fall quickly (gravity), but many do stay in the air and can travel across a room in a few seconds.

A single sneeze releases about 30,000 droplets, with droplets traveling at up to 200 miles per hour. Fig. 8.2 shows that most droplets are small and travel great distances (easily across a room).

If a person is infected, the droplets in a single cough or sneeze may contain as many as 200,000,000 (two hundred million) virus particles that can all be dispersed into the environment around them.

A single breath releases 50–5000 droplets. Most of these droplets are low velocity and fall to the ground quickly. There are even fewer droplets released through nose breathing. Importantly, due to the lack of exhalation force with a breath, viral particles from the lower respiratory areas are not expelled.

A cough or sneeze from a sick person, thus, puts out ~600 times more virus than normal breathing would do.

Droplets can fly and drift to about 6 feet away. They can be breathed in during that time, and they can land on surfaces. Aerosols are made up of smaller droplets and can travel 10–30 feet. Recent studies have shown that aerosols may be a common source of infection for COVID-19. Figure 8.2 shows this process.

**READ MORE**

[U8.1]   A description of how respiratory disease spread with some tentative numbers
[https://www.erinbromage.com/post/the-risks-know-them-avoid-them]

**TRANSMISSION**

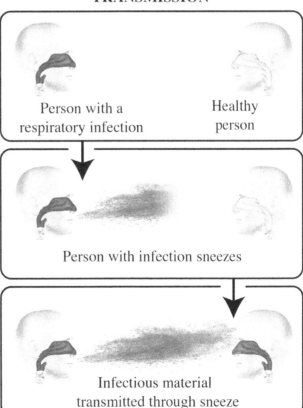

**Fig. 8.2** **[U8.2]** How a person with an infection spreads infectious material through sneezing to a healthy unprotected person. Movie by SLH. [http://stopTheSpread.health /TransmissionSneeze.mov]

## Coughing Can Also Be Passed by Hand

Fig. 8.3 shows that if you cough into your hand and then shake hands, the infection can end up on someone's face. The material coughed up can also land on someone else directly.

**Fig. 8.3** How infection can spread, from coughing into a hand, hand-shaking, to touching a face.

## How to Cough

To avoid having your droplets fly in the air and hit someone directly or contaminate a surface, you can cover your mouth.

Fig. 8.4 shows that the easiest solution is to wear a mask. On a more straightforward basis, you can cough into your sleeve (but will have to wash your shirt more often). You can also cough into a tissue or related paper product and then immediately dispose of the paper (or treat it as dirty). You should not cough directly into your hands.

## How Far Does a Sneeze Travel?

"The uncovered sneeze is the most dangerous breeze." —unknown

Sneezing is like a cough, but with more force. You should handle it the same way as a cough, but be aware it may spread farther. A video [U8.3] shows how far a sneeze can go. Sneezing is more dangerous than coughing because the velocity is much higher, and the particle size is broader, both larger and smaller. The particles go farther. Sneezing is an action particularly to avoid.

**LEARN MORE**

**[U8.3]** Video on how far can a sneeze go from the *Journal of the American Medical Association (JAMA)* [https://www.youtube.com/watch?v=piCWFgwysu0]

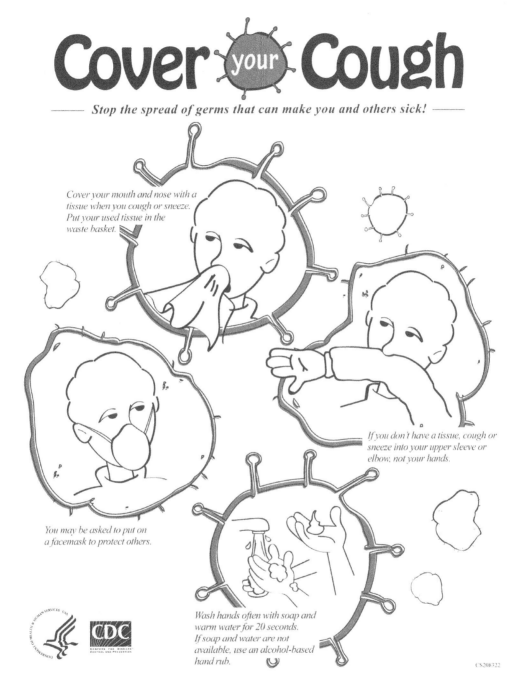

**Fig. 8.4** How to cover your cough and wear a mask and wash your hands to avoid spreading viruses.

## How to Sneeze

As Fig. 8.5 shows, like coughing, sneezing into a tissue is good form; sneezing into your hand is not appropriate.

If you are completely in your own space and no one visits you, then coughing and sneezing leading to infectious droplets is less of a concern. If you are in a public space, coughing and sneezing need to be covered.

**LEARN MORE**

**[U8.4]**  Mythbusters on sneezes
[https://www.youtube.com/watch?v=3vw0hIs2LEg]

**[U8.5]**  ABC News on sneezes
[https://www.youtube.com/watch?v=cQOSh6GLa_w]

**[U8.6]**  Search "How to cover your coughs and sneezes"

**Fig. 8.5** A correct way to sneeze is into a tissue.

## Summary of Social Distancing: Coughing and Sneezing Safely

This section explained why coughing and sneezing are so dangerous. Fig. 8.6 provides a visual example. Coughing and sneezing release large amounts of virus, perhaps 600 times what normal breathing does. This section noted several ways to directly reduce the effects of coughing and sneezing, including coughing into your sleeve and your shirt. Speaking, singing, and yelling can lead to the release of substantial amounts of viral particles, which can accumulate in a constrained space. Social distancing helps reduce the effects of coughs as well.

**Fig. 8.6** A man sneezing on a woman showing how far a sneeze can travel.

Masks, discussed in the next section, help reduce all of these sources. Once they are on, they provide more continuous protection to others and some protection to you too.

# Quiz 8: How to Cough and Sneeze

In this quiz, you will be given some general questions and some examples of how to sneeze, and asked to judge if they are appropriate and safe or not.

**Question 8.1**    **Can you cough into toilet paper if you do not have a tissue?**

A) Yes    B) No    C) Maybe

**Question 8.2**    **Can you cough into a bandana worn around your face?**

A) Yes    B) No    C) Maybe

**Question 8.3**    **Is this an appropriate way to cough or sneeze?**

A) Yes    B) No    C) Maybe

**Question 8.4**    **Is this an appropriate way to sneeze?**

A) Yes    B) No    C) Maybe

**Question 8.5**    **Is this an appropriate way to sneeze or cough?**

A) Yes    B) No    C) Maybe

**Question 8.6**     Did he cough correctly?

A) Yes     B) No     C) Maybe

**Question 8.7**     Is this an appropriate way to cough?

A) Yes     B) No     C) Maybe

**Question 8.8**     Is this an appropriate way to sneeze?

A) Yes     B) No     C) Maybe

**Question 8.9**   Is this an appropriate way to sneeze?

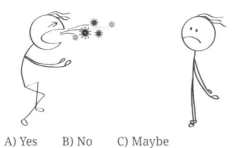

A) Yes      B) No      C) Maybe

**Question 8.10**   Should this be what your nose sees when you sneeze into a sleeve?

A) Yes      B) No      C) Maybe

**Question 8.11**   When this guy coughs, is it safe?

A) Yes      B) No      C) Maybe

## Answers to Quiz 8

**Question 8.1: A, Yes**
*Feedback:* Yes, using a piece of toilet paper as a tissue is good. This also might be very cost-effective.

**Question 8.2: A, Yes**
*Feedback:* Yes, coughing into a bandana is acceptable. But wash the bandana often; daily is a suggestion. The Internet has resources on how to use a bandana effectively and how to wash it. [U8.7] is a link to the CDC's recommendation on cleaning cloth face coverings (like bandanas).

**READ MORE**

**[U8.7]** CDC on how to clean cloth masks
[https://www.cdc.gov/coronavirus/2019-ncov/prevent-getting-sick/how-to-wash-cloth-face-coverings.html]

**Question 8.3: A, Yes**
*Feedback:* Yes. However, the virus may well be present on your elbow after coughing or sneezing and can survive for several hours to days. It is important to wash your clothes and have a bath at least once a day to get rid of the virus. It is not appropriate for sneezing because you need to cover your nose too!

**Question 8.4: A, Yes**
*Feedback:* Yes, using a tissue when sneezing will obstruct the spread. Just be sure to dispose of the tissue afterward and then wash your hands.

**Question 8.5: A, Yes**
*Feedback:* Yes, safe for others, but wash the shirt more often and try to find a tissue next time.

**Question 8.6: B, No**
*Feedback:* No, you should cough into a cloth (e.g., a sleeve or a tissue), or if unavailable, into your elbow like in question 8.3.

**Question 8.7: B, No**
*Feedback:* No, you should cough into a cloth (e.g., a sleeve or a tissue).

**Question 8.8: B, No**
*Feedback:* No, sneezing into your hand does not stop the spread of material unless you immediately wash your hands without touching anything else. Use a tissue, cloth, or sleeve instead.

**Question 8.9: B, No**
*Feedback:* No, sneezing at another person, even at six to ten feet, is not good practice for good hygiene or friendship.

**Question 8.10: A, Yes**
*Feedback:* Yes, if this is your sweatshirt—you are looking at a close up of a sleeve.

**Question 8.11: A, Yes**
*Feedback:* Yes, his mouth and nose are covered by a mask.

# 9

# Public PPE: Overview

## Overview of Public Personal Protective Equipment: Face Coverings, Eye Protection, and Gloves

This section introduces personal protective equipment for the public: face coverings, eye protection, and gloves, which are covered in the next three sections.

The CDC and the WHO recommend people voluntarily wear face coverings (masks), as shown in Fig. 9.1, when entering public spaces such as shopping centers and public transportation. Many people interested in stopping the spread and getting back to normal sooner are choosing to comply with the new guidelines. People concerned about their health also wear them. Experts suggest that the use of face masks is likely to continue. This section teaches you some basics.

You can use anything that covers your nose and mouth

**Fig. 9.1** People wearing different kinds of face coverings.

We will treat the phrase personal protective equipment (PPE) to mean equipment that protects individuals. The term PPE comes from the equipment medical, biological, and extreme environment researchers use, which we will not go over here. We will be talking about the less expensive and more available equipment that the public can use or even make. Primarily, this is masks or cloth face coverings. For ease of use, we will use the term "mask" and "cloth face covering" interchangeably, whereas it seems the CDC prefers the expression "cloth face covering."

**READ MORE**

[U9.1]  CDC overview of masks
[https://www.cdc.gov/coronavirus/2019-ncov/prevent-getting-sick/cloth-face-cover-guidance.html]

# Who Is Personal Protective Equipment For?

As the COVID-19 pandemic rapidly evolves, guidance from health officials has been updating and sometimes changing to reflect the situation as they study the disease and its effects, as Fig. 9.2 notes. In light of the new information, the CDC recommends that the general public use cloth face coverings, particularly in areas where it is difficult to maintain a safe distance and especially in geographic areas that are considered hot spots or where there is low ventilation.

**Fig. 9.2** As information is learned, there will be changes to recommendations, like now all people should wear cloth face coverings, not just people who are sick. Keep up with the latest information.

The reason for the change? The CDC has found recent studies showing that a significant number of people with COVID-19 lack symptoms (asymptomatic) and that even those who eventually develop symptoms (pre-symptomatic) can transmit the virus before any symptoms. That means that the virus can spread when people are in close contact (like going to the grocery store) through a simple sneeze, clearing of the throat, or even talking.

Health officials believe that wearing a cloth face covering is just one more way to do your part to help slow and stop the spread. As Fig. 9.3 notes, wearing a cloth face covering will protect those around you if you happen to be asymptomatic or pre-symptomatic.

**Fig. 9.3** Wearing a mask helps protect others around you.

**READ MORE**

[U9.2]  Don't just wear a mask for yourself
[https://www.theatlantic.com/health/archive/2020/04/dont-wear-mask-yourself/610336/]

# 10

# Public PPE: Masks

## Overview: What a Mask Does for You and Others

This section covers face coverings, also referred to as masks.

When you cough or sneeze, you can disperse particles quite a distance. There is also some evidence that singing, yelling, and even breathing disperse small particles that can have viruses in them. The virus in Fig. 10.1 would be stopped by a mask.

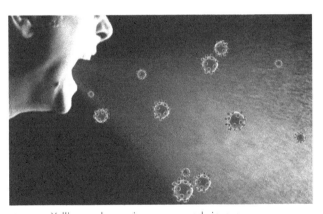

**Fig. 10.1** Yelling and sneezing can spread viruses.

A mask helps contain the droplets and reduces the amount of this dispersal (egress, particles escaping out from you). A mask also reduces what you take in (ingress, particles you take in), but this is seen as harder to do, and less important at this point. An added benefit to a mask is it decreases exposure of mucous membranes from touching your face—when paired with glasses, they create a good shield.

Both Dr. Fauci [U10.1] and Senate Majority Leader Mitch McConnell [U10.2] encourage you to wear masks.

[U10.1]   Dr. Fauci encourages you to wear a mask
[https://www.msn.com/en-us/news/politics/dr-fauci-i-wear-a-mask-because-its-effective/vi-BB1 4FyWz]

[U10.2]   Senator McConnell encourages you to wear a mask
[https://www.cnn.com/2020/07/09/politics/kentucky-circuit-judge-coronavirus-orders-masks /index.html]

**LEARN MORE**

**[U10.3]**    A video showing in a powerful way how a mask reduces the spread
[https://www.cnn.com/videos/health/2020/05/04/cough-coronavirus-masks-kaye-pkg-vpx.cnn]

**READ MORE**

**[U10.4]**    "Hey. Wear the damn mask." Explains why the wearing a mask reduces the spread of disease so
much
[https://www.cnn.com/2020/05/06/opinions/wear-the-damn-mask-pearlman/index.html]

**[U10.5]**    CDC overview of face coverings
[https://www.cdc.gov/coronavirus/2019-ncov/prevent-getting-sick/cloth-face-cover.html#studies]

## Types of Masks

There are several types of masks, as shown in Fig. 10.2. They vary in their cost, how easy they are to wear, how easy they are to clean, and if they are reusable. They vary in how you get them, and whether you buy them or make them. The different kinds and the different styles and manufacturers will fit you differently. You may need to try out several types to see which are most comfortable. You might also use different masks for different situations, e.g., a lightweight one for walking the dog where you do not meet many people, and a more heavy-duty one when shopping in a crowded store. Some masks are more efficient than others, but the best evidence from the best experts is that all are helpful [U10.7]. We next review the types.

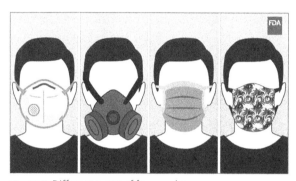

**Fig. 10.2** Different types of facemasks.

**READ MORE**

**[U10.6]**    What to look for in a mask
[https://fivethirtyeight.com/features/what-to-look-for-in-a-face-mask-according-to-science/]

**[U10.7]**    National Academy of Sciences, Engineering and Medicine report on how masks vary but all help:
Rapid expert consultation on the effectiveness of fabric masks for the COVID-19 pandemic
[https://www.nap.edu/download/25776]

## Types of Masks: N95 Respirators

Fig. 10.3 shows an N95 Respirator. This is the only type of (simple) mask that can actively stop an individual from breathing in most airborne and fluid hazards. The N95 mask is currently NOT part of the CDC's recommendations for the general public. What does the "N" and "95" mean? According to

**Fig. 10.3** An N95 mask.

the National Institute for Occupational Safety and Health (NIOSH), the "N" stands for "Not resistant to oil," and the "95" means "95% of airborne particles are filtered out." The version in Fig. 10.3 looks like it has an exhaust valve, which means that it would not filter the air you exhale.

These masks must be professionally fitted before wearing to work most effectively. They should be used by medical professionals who are caring for COVID-19 patients, scientists working with biohazards, or workers in hazardous environments. Some medical conditions can be worsened by wearing one of these masks (some heart and lung diseases, for example).

**LEARN MORE**

[U10.8]  How masks work
[https://www.youtube.com/watch?reload=9&v=eAdanPfQdCA]

## Types of Masks: Athletic Masks and Industrial Masks

There are two further types of masks to explain that do not always filter in both directions. (Masks that filter in both directions are safer.)

There are masks to restrict your breathing to help you train. Fig. 10.4 provides an example. If you have trouble breathing, these might not be for you. These masks typically filter air on the way in to make it harder to breathe so that you work harder. They do not always filter out, which does not protect others from your shedding. If you use one, you should adjust it so that it filters breath going out as well.

**Fig. 10.4** Athletic training facemask.

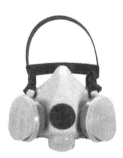

**Fig. 10.5** An industrial facemask.

There are also masks for working in dusty environments or near chemicals that only filter on the way in (military gas masks work this way as well), and you exhale through a valve that does not filter your breath going out. Fig. 10.5 provides an example. If you can fit a filter to this kind of mask to filter particles in both directions, it can provide a useful mask for use in a pandemic.

# Types of Masks: Surgical/Medical Masks

Fig. 10.6 shows an example of a standard surgical/medical mask. These are paper-like non-woven masks with elastic bands that wrap around your ears or strings that tie around the back of your head. These masks do not filter out as many particles as the N95 mask but are very helpful. If you would like a tighter fit to your mask, some folks are using tubes made from pantyhose to hold their masks closer to their face.

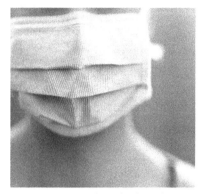

**Fig. 10.6** A surgical/medical mask.

Standard surgical masks protect against large droplet particles from spreading. This means they are effective in stopping cough droplets from a sick person from going outside the mask. You can find medical staff wearing these kinds of masks, and they are usually also given to patients with a cough who are in the waiting room at a doctor's office.

Standard surgical masks are not as effective as N95 masks in keeping dirty particles out of your mouth. But, wearing them helps stop the spread of COVID-19 by reducing particles going out and also reducing what comes in.

Surgeons wear these masks for hours, so they are okay to wear for a long time!

**READ MORE**

**[U10.9]**  Surgical masks can be very good on their own. Long, Youlin, Tengyue Hu, Liqin Liu, Rui Chen, Qiong Guo, Liu Yang, Yifan Cheng, Jin Huang, and Liang Du. 2020. "Effectiveness of N95 respirators versus surgical masks against influenza: A systematic review and meta-analysis." *Journal of Evidence-Based Medicine* 13 (2): 93-101. [https://pubmed.ncbi.nlm.nih.gov/32167245/]

# Types of Masks: Cloth Face Coverings

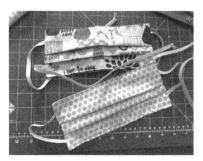

**Fig. 10.7** Two cloth masks.

Fig. 10.7 shows cloth face coverings or cloth masks, which are what the CDC currently recommends for people to use while in public places and what some local communities and stores are requiring in certain situations to keep infection rates from going up, as we come out of the shelter-in-place orders. Face coverings can be made of many different fabrics, with or without extra filters. Cloth face coverings can be inexpensive, easy to make, and stop particles from coming away from you but offer lower protection from breathing them in unless you pair them with a piece of nylon stockings or additional layers.

To encourage children to wear masks, you want to make it fun. These masks offer the greatest ability to provide fun masks for children (e.g., themed) and to make a fashion statement by having the mask match your outfit.

### READ MORE

[U10.10]  Adding a nylon stocking layer could boost protection from cloth masks, study finds
[https://www.npr.org/sections/goatsandsoda/2020/04/22/840146830/adding-a-nylon-stocking-layer
-could-boost-protection-from-cloth-masks-study-find]

[U10.11]  Dr. Fauci: I wear a mask because it is effective
[https://www.msn.com/en-us/news/politics/dr-fauci-i-wear-a-mask-because-its-effective/vi
-BB14FyWz]

### LEARN MORE

[U10.12]  US Surgeon General encourages mask wearing
[https://video.foxnews.com/v/6173226715001]

## How to Get a Mask

When it comes to getting a mask, you have a lot of different options. Fig. 10.8 notes several ways. Most likely, you already have something that will work as a mask in your house. Bandanas, scarfs, pashminas, and buffs (cloth tubes that can just be pulled over your nose and mouth) are just a few items people can find around their house. You can also find videos on how to make your own.

Search for "no-sew masks" if you are just looking for ideas on how to wrap or fold a cloth into a mask. Or, if you want to sew a mask, there are many designs and instructional videos to choose from. Fig. 10.9 shows some simple directions from the CDC to make your own no-sew mask with a piece of cloth or a bandana.

Many companies and individuals are also selling masks. Look online at Amazon, Etsy, or your favorite online shop. Also, check with your local

**Fig. 10.8** Community giveaways, DIY mask-making, and buying one are some ways to get a mask.

## Non-sewn Mask

### Materials

- Bandana, old t-shirt, or square cotton cloth (cut approximately 20"x20")
- Rubber bands (or hair ties)
- Scissors (if you are cutting your own cloth)

### Tutorial

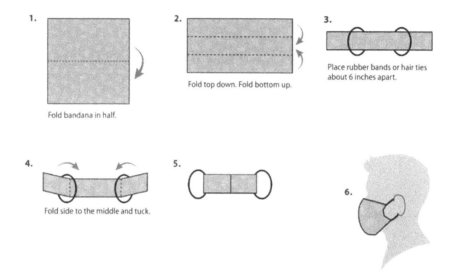

**Fig. 10.9** Follow these directions to make a no-sew mask.

government; they may have a place where they are giving them away. Stores increasingly sell them as well.

**READ MORE**

**[U10.13]**  CDC on how to make face coverings
[https://www.cdc.gov/coronavirus/2019-ncov/prevent-getting-sick/diy-cloth-face-coverings.html]

**[U10.14]**  Search more with Google:
[https://www.google.com/search?q=home-made+masks+for+covid]

**[U10.15]**  Search more with DuckDuckGo:
[https://duckduckgo.com/?t=ffab&q=home-made+masks+for+covid&ia=web]

**LEARN MORE**

**[U10.16]**  Two DIY mask designs based on using a t-shirt
[https://www.youtube.com/watch?v=r51YroAFPds]

# How to Put on Your Mask

Fig. 10.10 shows how to put on your mask: Some people are using a band-aid to make a seal around the bridge of their nose.

## MASK OR RESPIRATOR

- Secure ties or elastic bands at middle of head and neck
- Fit flexible band to nose bridge
- Fit snug to face and below chin
- Fit-check respirator

**Fig. 10.10** How to wear a mask.

**LEARN MORE**

[U10.17]  How to wear your mask
[https://www.youtube.com/watch?v=etZK-GrUYgM]

# How to Take off Your Mask

Fig. 10.11 shows the steps to remove a mask safely. For reusable masks, the point is to not touch the external surface and to place it in a way that you can pick it up and put it on without touching that surface again. Also, because

1. Clean your hands
2. Be careful not to touch your eyes, nose, or mouth while removing
3. Untie strings behind your head or stretch the ear loops to remove
4. Handle only by the ear loops or ties
5. Fold outside corners together
6. If the mask is to be re-used decide the best way to sanitize (time, heat, UV light, soap, washing machine, or disinfectant) or toss in the trash (if disposable)
7. Wash hands, again, immediately after removing

**Fig. 10.11** How to remove a mask.

the outer layer may be contaminated, it, and where it touches, will have to be disinfected by time, heat, or disinfectant.

Here is how to take off your mask:

1. Clean your hands
2. Only touching the straps, remove the mask (without touching the front of the mask)
3. If the mask is to be re-used, decide the best way to sanitize (time, heat, UV light, soap, or disinfectant)
4. Wash your hands again with soap or hand sanitizer

## Tips for Wearing Masks

Fig. 10.12 summarizes some tips for wearing, removing, and cleaning masks. Here are some more taken from the Read Mores in this subsection and our own use:

- It would be great if your cloth mask is made of multiple layers of fabric.

- The best practice is to put your mask on and take it off in your home.

- You might wish to keep a spare cloth mask for each person in your household in your car. If you forget, you have a spare ready to go. You might also keep some disposable masks there.

**Fig. 10.12** The letters M.A.S.K. provides a mnemonic for wearing a mask.

- Make sure the mask covers your nose and goes over your chin.
- Do not play with your mask; do not scratch your nose through or under the mask. These actions bring the mask more in touch with your face, and you touch your face as well.
- If you are hot in your mask (from CNN):
    a. Get out of the sun and into shade
    b. Pick a more breathable mask
    c. Bring a spare and swap masks
    d. Get a safe distance away from others and take it off for a break
- If your mask fogs up your glasses, here are several tips (from The Verge): Check the fit of your mask. Fog indicates a poor seal of the mask to your face.
    a. Put your mask on under your glasses
    b. If your mask does not have a bridge, you can make one using twist ties or pipe cleaners, or you can tape the mask down with tape or a band-aid.
    c. Wash your glasses with soapy water but let them dry with the soapy water on them. The soap film will help reduce fog. Avoid soaps made with lotion.
    d. Put a tissue inside of the mask to absorb and filter moisture
    e. Buy a commercial anti-fogging product
- If you have trouble breathing, feel dizzy, or your heart is racing, distance yourself from others, and take off your mask. You can also check the fit of your mask; it might be on incorrectly.
- Treat the front of the mask as possibly contaminated.
- When you remove your mask, remember not to touch your face, and remember then to wash your hands.
- Clean or replace your mask, either after each use or daily.
  To clean your mask: Wash cloth masks in a washing machine with any soap. Delicate fabrics or masks with washable filters may need to be hand-washed with soap. You can find out on the Internet how to use ovens, UV light, and other ways to clean masks.
- Fig. 10.13 shows a way to get your mask to fit more tightly using rubber bands based on [U10.18].
- What to do when people are not wearing masks? You have several choices. You can look at them in disgust. You can, if you feel comfortable, note to them that you are empathetic, but would feel safer if they wore a mask, or laugh at them, or you can leave the area. Arguing rarely works.

# RUBBER BAND METHOD TIGHTENS FACE MASK

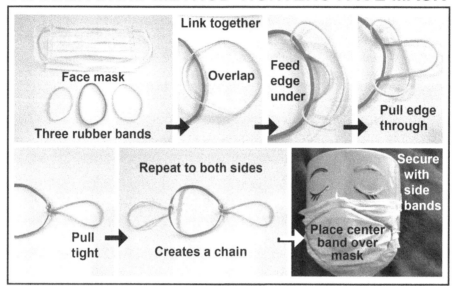

**Fig. 10.13** How to use three rubber bands to tighten a face mask.

**READ MORE**

**[U10.18]** How to use rubber bands to hold masks on more securely
[https://bestlifeonline.com/mask-hack-rubber-bands/]

**[U10.19]** How to wear masks in warm environments
[https://www.cnn.com/2020/06/10/health/wear-masks-summer-heat-sweat-wellness-trnd/index.html]

**[U10.20]** How to help avoid fogging your glasses while wearing a mask
[https://www.theverge.com/21301830/face-mask-glasses-fogging-how-to-stop-clear]

**[U10.21]** How to clean masks
[https://www.cnn.com/2020/06/08/cnn-underscored/how-to-clean-face-mask]

## When Not to Use Face Coverings

Not being able to wear a mask for health reasons is rare. However, as shown in Fig. 10.14, masks should not be placed on:

- Anyone with breathing issues
- Unconscious, incapacitated, or those otherwise unable to remove the mask on their own
- Children under the age of 2

**LEARN MORE**

**[U10.22]** Why and when to wear a cloth mask by Dr. McGraw, Director of Center for Infectious Disease Dynamics, Penn State
[https://news.psu.edu/video/618912/2020/05/06/when-and-why-should-i-wear-cloth-mask-ask-cidd]

# Not Everyone Should Wear a Mask

**Fig. 10.14** Some people who should not wear a mask are people with breathing issues, those with certain disabilities, and babies.

## Summary of Public PPE: Masks

This section has explained why to wear masks and what kinds of masks exist. It covered how to wear masks, and how to put them on, take them off, and clean them. This section also had some tips about how to do this more safely and comfortably.

Wearing a mask in crowded places is one of the simplest and easiest ways to protect yourself and to protect others in case you are asymptomatic. You cannot tell if you are asymptomatic, so unless you have had an antibody test that shows you have had COVID-19, or you have been sick with it, you cannot tell if you are asymptomatic. This is similar to looking before crossing a street or driving defensively near children. Nearly every time of every day, it is safe to cross most streets. Most times, a child will not follow a ball into the road. But on some days and some times you will protect yourself and others by looking. When should you look? You often do not know, so you have to every time. Wearing a mask is a sign of respect for others, like wearing a tie or a shirt and trousers.

You should also make it easy for yourself. Keep your mask by the door by your keys and a portable bottle of hand sanitizer.

Fig. 10.15 shows how more people wearing masks and wearing more efficient masks can help reduce transmission. As more of us wear masks, we reduce the spreading rate. If we choose more efficient masks, we can reduce the spread rate even further. For example, if only 25% of the population wore a perfect, 100% efficient mask, the transmission rate would be a little less than 3, indicating rapid spread. If about 40% wore 75% efficient masks, the transmission rate would be about 2. If 75% of the population (or more) wore masks that were 75% efficient, the transmission rate would be below 1, and the spread would slow down and stop.

# MASK WEARING AND MASK EFFICIENCY
## MORE PEOPLE DOING BOTH EQUALS LESS SPREAD

Numbered circles and coloring show average spread from a single case.
Note: Any number anything over 1 spreads exponentially.

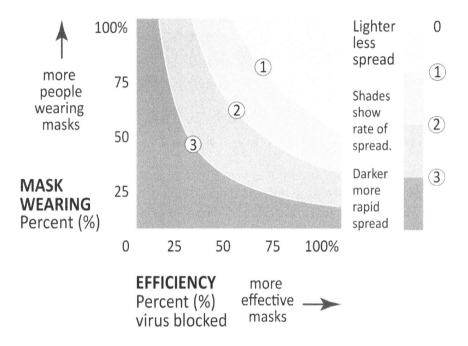

**Fig. 10.15** How mask-wearing and mask efficiency reduce the spread. Based on figure S4 from Tian et al., used with permission. [U10.23]

### READ MORE

[U10.23] Tian, Liang, Xuefei Li, Fei Qi, Qian-Yuan Tang, Viola Tang, Jiang Liu, Zhiyuan Li et al. 2020. "Calibrated intervention and containment of the COVID-19 pandemic." [https://arxiv.org/ftp/arxiv/papers/2003/2003.07353.pdf]

[U10.24] Masks help stop the spread of coronavirus – the science is simple and I'm one of 100 experts urging governors to require public mask-wearing [https://theconversation.com/masks-help-stop-the-spread-of-coronavirus-the-science-is-simple -and-im-one-of-100-experts-urging-governors-to-require-public-mask-wearing-138507]

[U10.25] *Atlantic* article on wearing masks [https://www.theatlantic.com/health/archive/2020/04/dont-wear-mask-yourself/610336/]

# Quiz 10: Face Masks on yourself and others

## Part 1: Proper face mask removal

This quiz is about removing your mask.

**Question 10.1**    Choose the Correct Order for Steps to Safely Removing a Mask

A) Only touching the straps, remove the mask (without touching the front of the mask)

B) Wash your hands with soap and water or hand sanitizer

C) Wash your hands with soap and water or hand sanitizer

D) If the mask is to be re-used, decide the best way to sanitize (time, heat, UV light, soap, or disinfectant) and put it in the right location

## Part 2: Are Other People Wearing Their Masks Correctly?

This quiz will help you identify if people are wearing their masks correctly. Each question refers to a picture by its corresponding alphabetical label (see page 92).

**Question 10.2**    Are the people labeled A-H wearing their masks correctly?

**i) Fig. 10.A**
A) Yes      B) No

**ii) Fig. 10.B**
A) Yes      B) No

**iii) Fig. 10.C**
A) Yes      B) No

**iv) Fig. 10.D**
A) Yes      B) No

**v) Fig. 10.E**
A) Yes      B) No

**vi) Fig. 10.F**
A) Yes      B) No

**vii) Fig. 10.G**
A) Yes      B) No

**viii) Fig. 10.H**
A) Yes      B) No

## Part 3: Cloth Face Coverings and PPEs

This quiz will help deepen your understanding of the masks/coverings that the general public can wear.

**Question 10.3**    If a healthcare worker is going to the grocery store, which mask(s) would be appropriate for them to use? (Pick all that apply)

A) Cloth mask
B) N95 facemask recently used in a hospital
C) Surgical facemask
D) Mask for woodworking

**Question 10.4**    Which would be the *least* helpful mask to use if a healthcare worker is going into the hospital and will be helping with COVID-19 patient intubations?

A) N95 facemask
B) Surgical facemask
C) Cloth mask
D) Positive air pressure mask for use with Ebola

**Question 10.5**    Should you wear a face covering if you are sick?

A) Yes      B) No       C) Maybe

**Question 10.6**    Should you cover your face if you are caring for a family member at home with COVID-19?

A) Yes      B) No       C) Maybe

**Question 10.7**    Does wearing a mask mean you can safely stand closer to people, hang out in large groups again, or finally gather with friends in their homes?

A) Yes      B) No       C) Maybe

**Answers to Quiz 10**

**Part 1: Proper Face Mask Removal**

**Question 10.1: B, A, D, C or C, A, D, B**
*Feedback:* The correct sequence should involve washing your hands before and after you carefully remove the mask and handling its disposal or sanitation appropriately.

**Part 2: Are Other People Wearing Their Masks Correctly?**

**Question 10.2: i) Yes, ii) Yes, iii) No, iv) No, v) No, vi) Yes, vii) No viii) Yes**
*Feedback:* i) Yes, everybody in this picture has their mask on covering their nose, mouth, chin, and no gaps. ii) Yes, Dick Cheney, in this picture, has his mask on covering his nose, mouth, chin, and no gaps. iii) No, this man is wearing an eye shield only. He will be protected from spray, but not inhaling particles. iv) No, the mask should not be worn under the chin. It should cover your nose, mouth, and chin and have no gaps. v) No, this mask is not protecting him because it is not on or tied. vi) Yes, this mask is over the nose, mouth, and chin and has no gap. vii) No, this mask has holes where his mouth is and will not block particles if he coughs. viii) Yes, this is an excellent use of a scarf as a face covering. It is covering his nose, mouth, and chin and has no gaps.

**Part 3: Cloth Face Coverings and PPEs**

**Question 10.3: A, Cloth mask, and C, Surgical Facemask**
*Feedback:* A and C are all appropriate, while B and D are not. They should save the higher-level masks for use in a healthcare facility, and a woodworking mask typically has vents, so they do not filter what you exhale.

**Question 10.4: C, Cloth mask**
*Feedback:* C, a cloth mask would be the least helpful for a healthcare worker that works with COVID-19 patients. A cloth mask helps you from infecting others, but helping intubate a COVID-19 patient poses significant risks for those helping and performing the intubation.

**Question 10.5: A, Yes**
*Feedback:* Yes. If you are sick: You should wear a face mask, if available, when you are around other people, including before you enter a health care provider's office or if someone comes into your room at home to care for you.

**READ MORE**

**[U10.26]** CDC on how and to wear a mask when sick
[https://www.cdc.gov/coronavirus/2019-ncov/prevent-getting-sick/cloth-face-cover-faq.html]

**Question 10.6: A, Yes**
*Feedback:* Yes, if you are caring for others. If the person who is sick is not able to wear a face mask (for example, because it causes trouble breathing), then as their caregiver, you should wear a face mask when in the same room with them. If they can wear a mask, it is still in your interest to wear a mask yourself. Visitors, other than caregivers, are not recommended.

**READ MORE**

[U10.27] CDC on why to wear a mask when caring for someone who is sick
[https://www.cdc.gov/coronavirus/2019-ncov/if-you-are-sick/care-for-someone.html]

**Question 10.7: B, No**

*Feedback:* No, wearing a mask in public is not a substitute for social distancing, quarantining, handwashing, or avoiding touching your face. Wearing a mask is meant to be an additional effort to slow and stop the spread, not a replacement to what we already have in place. All these activities help reduce the spread and do not replace each other.

# 11: Public PPE: Eye Protection

## Wearing Eye Protection

It is known that the Coronavirus can enter through our mucous membranes, which includes our eyes.

The CDC recommends eye protection for healthcare workers in health care settings (19 July 2020). They do not discuss any recommendations outside of the healthcare setting.

Our recommendation is to consider wearing eye covering (Fig. 11.1 shows some examples) when you are more at risk or when you are in larger crowds. Where the disease is transmitted by droplets in the air, eye protection can help reduce this factor. Eye protection can also help remind you not to touch your face.

Eye care experts have suggested reconsidering the use of wearing contact lenses during the pandemic. There is no evidence suggesting wearing contact lenses increases your risk of contracting the virus; however, experts reason that people who wear contact lenses touch their eyes more than the average non-contact wearer. So, wearing glasses might provide an additional way not to touch your eyes, as a further warning (reminder) that you should not touch your eyes. Substituting glasses for contact lenses may also help by providing a barrier between your hands and your eyes. This same idea could be used for wearing a face shield and sunglasses too. It can be considered a physical barrier reminder to keep your fingers away from your eyes.

Wearing glasses may also provide a barrier for respiratory droplets, but remember, this is not a guarantee. Virus droplets could still get in through the sides, top, and bottoms of glasses; a face shield may provide

**Fig. 11.1** The virus can enter through your eyes, a mucous membrane. Wearing glasses or face shields are two ways to protect your eyes better when out in public. Contact lenses may lead you to touch your eyes more often, so be mindful of keeping your hands clean.

more coverage. If you are caring for a sick patient in your home, swim or ski goggles or a face shield could give a better defense and have been used in hospitals. But the best defense is to practice social distancing and continue to practice good hygiene habits, like washing your hands and following the recommendations from the CDC.

**READ MORE**

[U11.1]   NPR on why you might want to protect your eyes
[https://www.npr.org/sections/goatsandsoda/2020/05/22/861299427/coronavirus-faqs-can-i-catch-it
-through-the-eyes-will-googles-help]

## Quiz 11: Eye and Face Protection

The quiz you are about to take summarizes and tests your knowledge on what information we know currently about eye and face protection during the coronavirus pandemic.

**Question 11.1**  So far, we know the coronavirus can enter into a host through mucous membranes. Are your eyes considered a mucous membrane?

A) Yes    B) No    C) Maybe

**Question 11.2**  Does the CDC recommend everyone wear face shields to protect their eyes?

A) Yes    B) No    C) Maybe

**Question 11.3**  Can contact lenses give me the coronavirus?

A) Yes    B) No    C) Maybe

**Question 11.4**  If you are going out on a walk outside in public and have been generally healthy, do you need to wear a face mask?

A) Yes    B) No    C) Maybe

**Question 11.5**  True or false: If you are not a medical professional or other essential worker, you probably do not need an N95 Respirator.

A) True    B) False

## Answers to Quiz 11

**Question 11.1: A, Yes**
*Feedback:* Yes, the eyes are part of your mucous membranes. If you get infectious respiratory droplets in your eye, you could be infected.

**Question 11.2: B, No**
*Feedback:* No, the CDC is recommending only healthcare workers in healthcare facilities wear protection for their eyes, though face shields do offer an additional layer of protection. This appears to be changing, so check with the CDC website or your healthcare provider.

**Question 11.3: B, No**
*Feedback:* No, there is no evidence that contact lenses can give you the coronavirus on their own. However, people who wear contact lenses have been known to touch their eyes more and should clean their hands more often.

**Question 11.4: B, No**
*Feedback:* No, social distancing will provide enough protection. In case you end up in a crowd, it would be wise to carry a mask. Local rules may require a mask as a backup in case you end up within social distance. If you are following someone who is exercising heavily or running, then you may wish to separate by 15 feet or more.

**READ MORE**

[U11.2]    Report on social distancing and exercising
           [http://www.urbanphysics.net/Social%20Distancing%20v20_White_Paper.pdf]

[U11.3]    Another report on social distancing and exercising
           [https://bgr.com/2020/04/09/coronavirus-outdoors-exercise-social-distancing]

**Question 11.5: A, True**
*Feedback:* True. N95 Respirators should be reserved for essential workers who are working with sick patients or on the advice of your healthcare provider.

# 12

# Public PPE: Gloves

## Wearing Gloves

This section discusses whether to wear gloves and how to do so if you choose to wear them.

The CDC recommends wearing one layer of medical examination gloves in healthcare settings, like those in Fig. 12.1. For non-healthcare workers, your skin does a great job protecting you from most respiratory infections acquired through touching things as long as you remember to wash your hands before touching your face.

**Fig. 12.1** Disposable gloves can be useful if you have cuts on your hands or if they remind you not to touch your face.

The CDC does not discuss wearing gloves outside the healthcare setting. For those outside a healthcare setting, the CDC recommends social distancing and staying at home as much as possible. Wearing gloves when making trips to the grocery store can help prevent the spread of infection onto hands. However, the gloves would need to be changed or washed or sanitized each time you touch something new (car door handle, steering wheel, the items you touch at the grocery store, or keys) and might touch your face or something you eat.

If wearing gloves helps you remember not to touch your face, then wear gloves. If you have cuts or scratches on your hands, wear gloves if you are out in public. Because of these reasons and the shortage of medical supplies for our healthcare workers, it is best to practice proper handwashing and social distancing instead of single-use gloves.

# How to Put Gloves On

Follow the steps below to put on gloves properly:

1. Take off any jewelry.
2. Wash hands.
3. Inspect gloves for tears, discoloration, or dampness (discard if gloves are compromised). Make sure they are the correct size (Fig. 12.2).
4. Place the glove on the dominant hand, being careful only to touch only the inside part of the glove.
5. Slip hand into the glove, palm up and fingers open.
6. Repeat with the other hand.
7. Adjust gloves up and make sure to cover wrists.

**Fig. 12.2** If wearing a disposable glove, you should choose the correct sized glove for your hand. Not too tight or loose.

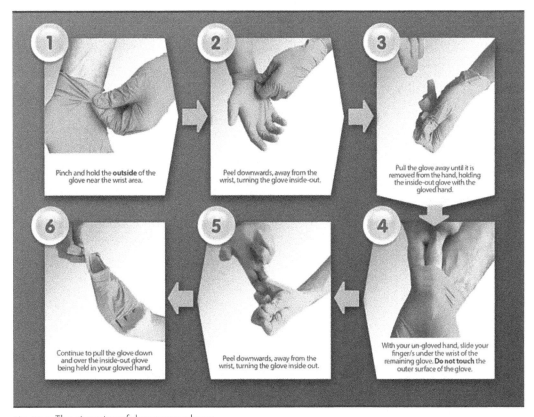

1. Pinch and hold the **outside** of the glove near the wrist area.

2. Peel downwards, away from the wrist, turning the glove inside-out.

3. Pull the glove away until it is removed from the hand, holding the inside-out glove with the gloved hand.

4. With your un-gloved hand, slide your finger/s under the wrist of the remaining glove. **Do not touch** the outer surface of the glove.

5. Peel downwards, away from the wrist, turning the glove inside out.

6. Continue to pull the glove down and over the inside-out glove being held in your gloved hand.

**Fig. 12.3** The steps to safely remove gloves.

# How to Remove Gloves

The point in removing gloves is not to contaminate yourself as you remove them. Fig. 12.3 (previous page) shows the steps. If you can, wash or sanitize your hands with the gloves on. This will help reduce the chance of contamination if you make a mistake.

You should first test the gloves to see if the sanitizer or washing hurts them.

And remember, while wearing the gloves always:

- Keep hands away from face/eyes
- Change gloves at least between the public space you are going to (i.e., grocery store) and the private place you are returning to (your car or home)

And remember to clean your hands afterward, as Fig. 12.4 shows.

**WASH HANDS OR USE AN ALCOHOL-BASED HAND SANITIZER IMMEDIATELY AFTER REMOVING ALL PPE**

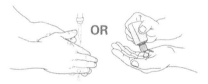

**Fig. 12.4** Remember to clean hands after removing PPE.

# Quiz 12: Gloves

This quiz summarizes this section on gloves by asking questions about wearing gloves.

**Question 12.1**    **What is the correct sequence for putting on gloves?**

A) Choose the properly sized glove for your hand. Not too tight or loose
B) Place the glove on the dominant hand, being careful only to touch only the inside part of the glove
C) Slip hand into the glove, palm up and fingers open
D) Take off any jewelry
E) Repeat with the other hand
F) Wash hands
G) Inspect gloves for tears, discoloration, or dampness (discard if gloves are compromised)
H) Adjust gloves up and make sure to cover wrists

**Question 12.2**    **Can wearing gloves to the grocery store help protect me from the Coronavirus?**

A) Yes    B) No    C) Maybe

**Question 12.3**    **Can I use winter gloves for protection when opening my car door?**

A) Yes    B) No    C) Maybe

**Question 12.4**    **If I am sick, can I use gloves and go to work and not worry about spreading it to other people?**

A) Yes    B) No    C) Maybe

**Question 12.5**    **I have a big cut on my hand. Should I wear gloves to protect myself?**

A) Yes    B) No    C) Maybe

**Question 12.6**    **Can I keep gloves on and clean them with hand sanitizer when I transition between places?**

A) Yes    B) No    C) Depends on the material of the glove

**Question 12.7**    **Does the CDC recommend that we wear gloves when going out shopping?**

A) Yes    B) No    C) Maybe

## Answers to Quiz 12

**Question 12.1: A, D, F, G, B, C, E, H**
*Feedback:* Wearing gloves correctly requires you to carefully maintain their cleanliness and integrity while putting them one. Ensuring you have a proper fit, starting with clean, unadorned hands, and carefully putting the gloves on will all help you stay safe.

**Question 12.2: A, Yes**
*Feedback:* Yes, wearing gloves can provide an additional barrier for your skin, but they are not perfect. If you let your guard down and touch your face or phone while wearing gloves, they are not fully helping.

**Question 12.3: A, Yes**
*Feedback:* Yes, but remember, if you do not take your gloves off when inside your car, then the gloves can be transferring whatever was on your door to the next object you touch and so you want to be very mindful about what you touch.

**Question 12.4: B, No**
*Feedback:* No, gloves will not be enough protection for others if you are infected. The best course of action if you are infected is to stay isolated and not be in contact with others. If you are near others while infected, wear a mask.

**Question 12.5: A, Yes**
*Feedback:* Yes, you can wear gloves, or another idea that might be easier is to wear a bandage to protect the wound from infection. Do not forget to wash your hands as you transition from one place to another.

**Question 12.6: C, Depends on the material of the glove**
*Feedback:* Whether it is safe to clean your gloves with sanitizer depends on the material of the glove. You would have to check what the gloves are made out of and make sure that there would be no chemical reaction that could damage the glove or that the surface can be cleaned with a sanitizer (woollen mittens, for example, cannot easily be disinfected).

**Question 12.7: B, No**
*Feedback:* No, at this time, the CDC does not recommend that the general public wear gloves. They do recommend gloves be worn in healthcare settings.

# 13

# Washing: Hands and More

## Overview of Washing Hands

You might think you know how to wash your hands. Numerous posters remind us to do so (Fig. 13.1). But, we do not always do an effective job. For example, young nursing students are often put through an exercise where someone smears a lotion on their hands that is only visible with black (UV) light. They are then told to wash their hands. Once they wash their hands, they then hold them under the UV light. Often, traces of the lotion can still be seen, particularly by their fingernails and back of hands, as shown in Fig. 13.2.

**Fig. 13.1** CDC posters to remind you to wash your hands.

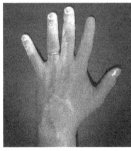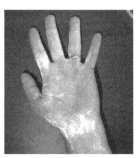

**Fig. 13.2** White glowing areas on the top (left) and bottom (right) of hands show where UV sensitive lotion was missed after hand washing.

This exercise demonstrates how to wash your hands thoroughly. Routinely, the nursing students learn to wash their hands longer and more carefully. If you do not wash your hands thoroughly for 20 seconds when you wash them, you can find commonly missed areas like your fingertips and cuticle areas, as shown specifically in Fig. 13.2 and, generally, in Fig. 13.3.

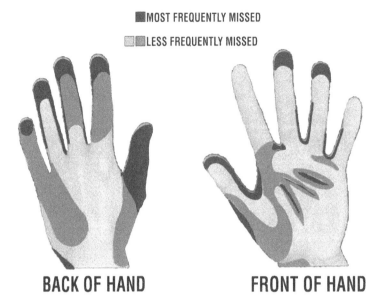

**MOST FREQUENTLY MISSED**

**LESS FREQUENTLY MISSED**

**BACK OF HAND**          **FRONT OF HAND**

**Fig. 13.3** Illustration showing areas of the hand that are frequently missed after hand washing, darker areas are more frequently missed*.

This section teaches you the details of washing your hands. Washing your hands can be an important aspect of protecting yourself and thus the people around you and flattening the curve. A recent study** estimates that improving the rates of handwashing by travelers passing through just 10 of the world's leading airports could significantly reduce the spread of many infectious diseases. And the greater the improvement in people's handwashing habits at airports, the more dramatic the effect on slowing diseases.

## Why Wash Hands and What to Not Touch with Your Hands

The skin on your hands serves as a great barrier to infections while allowing you to interact with the world. But, your hands have a habit of touching other surfaces and thus can get infectious material on them. When they touch other surfaces, they transfer this material, which often does not need a high concentration to be infectious. Then, when they touch your head, particularly the mucous membranes on your head, you can become infected.

---

* Taylor, L. J. (1978). An evaluation of handwashing techniques-1, *Nursing Times*. 74(2): 54-5.
** Christos Nicolaides, Demetris Avraam, Luis Cueto-Felgueroso, Marta C. Gonzalez, Rubin Juanes. Hand-hygiene mitigation strategies against global disease spreading through the air transportation network. Risk Analysis, 2019, DOI: 10.1111/risa.13428

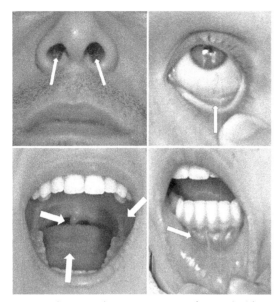

**Fig. 13.4** Arrows point to mucous membranes inside the nostrils, eyelid, and mouth and inner lip.

Washing your hands often reduces the number of times they transfer material and makes them cleaner when you touch the mucous membranes, particularly those found on your face. Mucous membranes secrete a thick protective fluid, mucus, designed to help stop pathogens and dirt from entering the body and to prevent tissue dehydration. Fig. 13.4 shows the locations of the mucous membranes on your head. Your lungs and the pathway to them are also mucous membranes.

These places should not be touched without cleaning your hands first because what is on your hands can get directly into your body this way.

Here is another way to imagine your mucous membranes. If touching that part of your body with spicy pepper sauce would hurt, that is a mucous membrane.

**LEARN MORE**

**[U13.1]** A nurse shows what cross-contamination is and how it happens
[https://www.youtube.com/watch?v=6iFjNXUvGwE]

# Other Types of Skin Openings

In addition to your mucous membranes, infectious agents can get into your body through wounds and other holes in your skin. Examples are shown in Fig. 13.5. These include abrasions (rubbed off skin), lacerations (cuts), and punctures (holes). It is crucial to clean and cover these as soon as possible.

If you are out in public or are otherwise exposed to infectious agents like

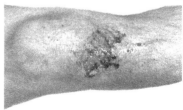

**Fig. 13.5** Skin cuts, abrasions, and other injuries need to be cleaned and covered to prevent infectious agents from entering the body.

bacteria and viruses, you should cover any skin openings to provide a barrier and work to heal them as soon as you can. If you have broken skin on your hands, then that is a good reason to wear gloves.

## Steps to Clean Wounds

If you do have a wound, you should clean and protect it as soon as possible to prevent infection.

1. Wash your hands with the steps given earlier in this section. Your hands must be clean when working on an open wound. Gloves are great as well, but not necessary when coming into contact with your own blood.
2. Run the wound under warm water to clean the wound.
3. Prepare a piece of sterile gauze or bandage. If you have to set the bandage down, allow the dressing to lay in its packaging, as shown in Fig. 13.6.
4. Apply the dressing onto the wound and secure with tape or the sticky sides of the bandage.

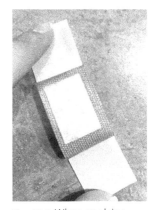

**Fig. 13.6** When applying an adhesive bandage, only touch the paper backing.

## When to Wash Your Hands

The CDC recommends that you can help yourself and your loved ones stay healthy by washing your hands often. But, when is that, and how often?

The times to wash your hands can be represented as when they are dirty, when you touch high-touch objects, and before or after you do important activities. In the first case, you should wash your hands when they are visibly dirty.

In the second case, touching things in your environment that other people touch can make your hands dirty. Fig. 13.7 shows some examples. Here are some more: Money, cell phones, eyeglasses, keys, nail clippers not yet cleaned, coins, car handles, gas pumps, car steering wheels, the floor, banisters, toys, laptops, counters, papers, contracts, door handles, food not yet prepared, or other people's hands. Board games and cards from card games can also be high-touch objects if used by people outside your household.

Some things are clean and safe to touch. Examples include soap, paper products (toilet paper, tissues, paper towels) fresh from their containers, wipes, and the inside of bandages before they are used.

**Fig. 13.7** Times to wash your hands: after touching a cell phone, sharing a credit card with someone else, and shopping.

So, clean your hands after touching the items that can dirty your hands and certainly before touching your face, other mucous membranes, or things you eat.

If you touch a contaminated surface, such as a table or a light switch, then you will have that contamination on the part of your body where you touched it. If it is a sleeve, it is on your sleeve. If it is your hand, it is on your hand. A way to get the contamination off is to wash your garment or to wash your hands. The most common thing you touch your face with is your hand, so washing your hands matter.

In the third case, you should wash your hands before or after important activities.

### Before, During, and After

- Preparing food

### Before

- Eating food

### Before and After

- Using the toilet (before if you will touch a mucous membrane)
- Treating a cut or wound
- Caring for someone at home, particularly who is sick with vomiting or diarrhea

### After

- Changing diapers or cleaning up a child who has used the toilet
- Blowing your nose, coughing, or sneezing
- Touching an animal, animal feed, or animal waste
- Handling pet food or treats
- Touching garbage
- Coming in from outside the home

**READ MORE**

**[U13.2]**  Aiello, Allison E., Rebecca M. Coulborn, Vanessa Perez, and Elaine L. Larson. 2008. "Effect of hand hygiene on infectious disease risk in the community setting: A meta-analysis." *American J of Public Health* 98 (8): 1372-1381.
[https://pubmed.ncbi.nlm.nih.gov/18556606/]

# Steps on How to Wash Your Hands: Description and Diagram

You might think you know how to wash your hands. The truth is that most people do not wash their hands carefully [U13.3] or long enough to prevent an infection. With a serious infection around, it is worth picking up your game by washing your hands more carefully and completely.

Here are the steps on "How to Wash Your Hands" (from the CDC):

1. Wet your hands with clean, running water (warm or cold), turn off the tap, and apply soap.
2. Lather your hands by rubbing them together with the soap. Lather the backs of your hands, between your fingers, and under your nails.
3. Scrub your hands for at least 20 seconds. Need a timer? Hum the "Happy Birthday" song from beginning to end twice.
4. Turn on the faucet. If you do not have a clean towel/paper towel to turn the faucet off, now would be a good time to take your soaped up hands and wash the faucet to keep from re-contaminating your hands when you turn the faucet off.
5. Rinse your hands well under clean, running water.
6. Pick up a clean towel/paper towel to turn faucet off. (You can also use it to open a door!)
7. Dry your hands using a clean towel or air-dry them.

**READ MORE**

**[U13.3]**  Study revealing that 95 percent of people failed to wash their hands correctly after using the bathroom
[https://msutoday.msu.edu/news/2013/eww-only-5-percent-wash-hands-correctly/]

**LEARN MORE**

**[U13.4]**  Nursing professor teaches how to wash hands
[https://youtu.be/1AGW3bbcb3Y]

**[U13.5]**  CDC explains how to wash hands
[https://www.cdc.gov/healthywater/hygiene/hand/handwashing.html]

# More Details on Washing Hands

Fig. 13.8 from the World Health Organization (WHO) provides another, more detailed viewpoint, particularly of step 3 of scrubbing your hands, showing you more about how to spend the 20 seconds washing your hands:

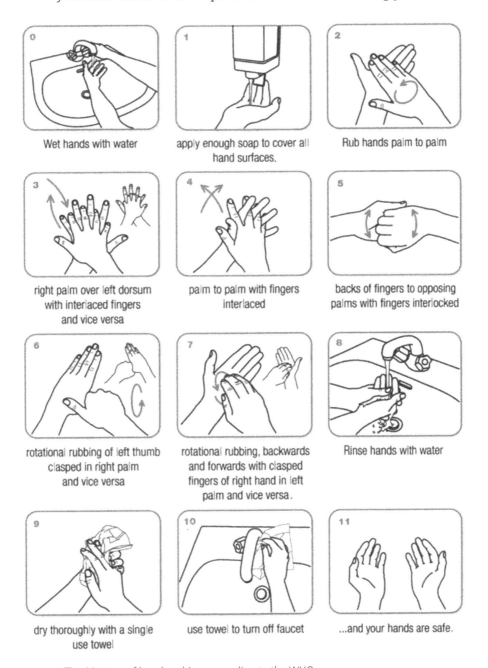

**Fig. 13.8** The 11 steps of handwashing, according to the WHO.

## How to Dry Hands

After you wash your hands, you are not done. You have to dry them as well. You can also let them air dry, but while they are wet, they can pick up infectious material more easily [U13.6].

There are two good ways to dry your hands. One is with an air dryer. The other is with a disposable towel or a towel that has only been used to dry clean hands.

The advantage of using a disposable towel is that you can then use it to turn off the water and open a door if you are in a bathroom (thus, garbage cans should be near the door in a bathroom).

**READ MORE**

**[U13.6]**   The CDC on handwashing
[https://www.cdc.gov/handwashing/show-me-the-science-handwashing.html]

## Theory of Soap: To Cut Oil and Grease and Allow Water to Wash Away Germs

Knowing how soap works will help you use it more confidently. Soap is a salt of fatty acids that allows grime and oils to be emulsified and thus able to be washed away with water. Emulsification is the process that allows two liquids that do not mix, such as oil and water, to be mixed. The soap particles latch one end on to the oil and one end to the water. More water can then carry away the combination.

In addition to removing dirt and oil, soap is particularly effective at killing the coronavirus because it is encased in a fatty layer, which soap destroys. Soap is better at killing the coronavirus than bleach, alcohol, hand sanitizer, and disinfectants (which also deactivate it).

Per the FDA, any soap works against the coronavirus. There is no additional benefit to anti-bacterial or other special soaps [U13.7].

Detergents are also emulsifiers for oil and water but are chemically different from soaps, and typically are stronger. Detergents are also highly effective against the coronavirus.

Hair conditioners are not soap and are not effective against the coronavirus. Shampoos are soap-like, however, and can be used if necessary.

**READ MORE**

**[U13.7]**   Soaps that kill the COVID-19 virus
[https://www.fda.gov/consumers/consumer-updates/antibacterial-soap-you-can-skip-it-use-plain-soap-and-water]

## Avoiding Physical Contact Completely

Another way to avoid getting your hands dirty is not to touch things. This skill is not often directly discussed, but we think it should be.

If you can go through a door (door 1 in Fig.13.9) that automatically opens or turn on a light without touching it with your hands, then you do not have to worry about your hands getting dirty, and then about cleaning your hands.

You might thus seek out bathrooms without doors (or with propped open doors or automatic doors), or automatic sinks, or buttons that you can hit the outside of your elbow to open doors (door 2 in Fig. 13.9).

In high traffic areas and where you can safely leave a door open (e.g., no fire code or safety considerations), you might leave a door ajar (door 2 in Fig. 13.9) so that people can open it with their feet or use a touchless handle.

Thus, when you can use your foot to open a door at the bottom, push a door with your back, use an automatic door opener, use your sleeve or a tissue to open a door or push a button or wait for someone to push on the other side, you should consider doing so.

A side effect of this is that you will have to wash your clothes that you use in this way more often, and treat them as a high-touch surface.

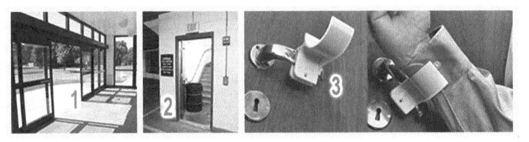

**Fig. 13.9** Doors that do not have to be opened are better, including sliding doors (1), doors propped open (2), and door handles fit with extensions to open with an arm instead of a hand (3).

## Summary of Washing Hands

At this point, you should now know why to wash your hands. It removes dirt and, particularly in a pandemic, infectious material. Ordinary soap will kill the SARS-CoV-2 virus, so washing with plain soap is enough. You now know what types of soap work: nearly all of them.

You should know when to wash your hands. In particular, before eating, after leaving a public area, and after touching high-touch surfaces. You may wish to take handwashing a step further and take a shower and put on clean clothes when you have been in a particularly risky location, such as a crowded store, a hospital, or a large gathering.

You now should know how to wash your hands and to wash for 20 seconds when you wish them to be particularly clean. Here, we would note that washing your wrists and exposed arms could be a good idea when they are dirty. You should know how to dry your hands, and how drying them with a paper towel can facilitate opening bathroom doors.

If you want your children to want to wash their hands more often, you can get soap with themes for children or soap with a toy or money inside.

We end this section with a quiz about when to wash your hands and the theory of washing your hands.

# Quiz 13: Washing Hands and More

## Part 1: Mucous Membranes

Here are some questions about mucous membranes. Can you recognize them and reason about how to protect them?

**Question 13.1**    **Which are examples of mucous membranes?**

A) Inside of the nose
B) Inside the mouth
C) Skin on the back of the hand

**Question 13.2**    **Do contact lenses make contact with mucous membranes?**

A) Yes    B) No    C) Maybe

**Question 13.3**    **Why should you wash your hands before eating, even if they do not look dirty?**

A) You heard it in a movie
B) Smells on your hand can transfer to the food
C) Viruses and bacteria are not visible to the naked eye

**Question 13.4**    **Does a paper cut count as a break in the skin?**

A) Yes    B) No    C) Maybe

**Question 13.5**    **Can you get COVID-19 by picking your teeth? My teeth are hard and not mucousy!**

A) Yes    B) No    C) Maybe

## Part 2: When to Wash Your Hands

Here are a series of questions to test your knowledge about the best time to wash your hands, and how to make sure you wash them properly.

**Question 13.6a**  **Do your hands need to be washed after opening this push door?**

A) Yes    B) No    C) Maybe

**Question 13.6b**  Do your hands need to be washed after opening the previous push door, if it was spray sanitized first?

A) Yes    B) No    C) Maybe

**Question 13.7**  To avoid catching a disease, should you wash your hands after touching a light switch cleaned with a dry tissue in your house, where you live alone?

A) Yes    B) No    C) Maybe

**Question 13.8**  To avoid catching a disease, should you wash your hands after touching an unknown light switch at work?

A) Yes    B) No    C) Maybe

**Question 13.9**  To avoid catching a disease, should you wash your hands after touching an unknown light switch in an unoccupied house that has not had visitors for two weeks?

A) Yes    B) No    C) Maybe

**Question 13.10**  Should you wash your hands when you come in from outside?

A) Yes    B) No    C) Maybe

Part 3: Washing your hands properly

**Question 13.11**  Order these steps in the correct order for washing your hands

A) Wet your hands with clean, running water (warm or cold), turn off the tap, and apply soap.
B) Rinse your hands well under clean, running water.
C) Lather your hands by rubbing them together with the soap. Lather the backs of your hands, between your fingers, and under your nails.
D) Pick up a clean towel/paper towel to turn the faucet off, which you can also use to open the door.
E) Dry your hands using a clean towel or air-dry them.
F) Scrub your hands for at least 20 seconds. Need a timer? Hum the "Happy Birthday" song from beginning to end twice.

**Question 13.12**  How long should you wash your hands?

A) 5 seconds
B) 10 seconds
C) 15 seconds
D) 20+ seconds

**Question 13.13**   Which is the best way to dry hands?

A) With a clean hand towel
B) With a clean paper towel
C) Air dryer
D) Any of the above

**Question 13.14**   Can you re-contaminate your hands immediately after washing them by touching the bathroom door?

A) Yes        B) No        C) Maybe

**Question 13.15**   Can you wash the faucet or the door handle while you wash your hands?

A) Yes        B) No        C) Maybe

**Question 13.16**   Can you re-contaminate your hands immediately after washing them by touching the faucet to turn it off?

A) Yes        B) No        C) Maybe

**Question 13.17**   Can you re-contaminate your hands immediately after washing them by having them touch each other?

A) Yes        B) No        C) Maybe

**Question 13.18**   Can you re-contaminate your hands immediately after washing them by picking up something from the floor?

A) Yes        B) No        C) Maybe

## Part 4: What Soaps Are Effective for Washing Hands?

This section checks whether you can pick which soaps would be effective for washing your hands.

**Question 13.19**  In photo A, can you use this sink to wash your hands?

A) Yes    B) No    C) Maybe

**Question 13.20**  Can you use the product (facial soap) in photo B to wash your hands?

A) Yes    B) No    C) Maybe

**Question 13.21**  Can you use the product (shampoo) in photo C to wash your hands?

A) Yes    B) No    C) Maybe

**Question 13.22**  Can you use the product (liquid soap) in photo D to wash your hands?

A) Yes    B) No    C) Maybe

**Question 13.23**  Can you use the product (petroleum jelly) in photo E to wash your hands?

A) Yes    B) No    C) Maybe

**Question 13.24**  Can you use the product (wipes) in photo F to wash your hands?

A) Yes    B) No    C) Maybe

**Question 13.25**  Can you use the product in photo G to wash your hands or face? (It says "not a soap" on the box on the right)

A) Yes    B) No    C) Maybe

**Question 13.26**  Can you use skin or cold cream like in photo H to wash your hands or face?

A) Yes    B) No    C) Maybe

**Question 13.27**  Can you use the product (disinfectant wipes) in photo I to wash your hands?

A) Yes    B) No    C) Maybe

**Question 13.28**  Is liquid soap from public bathrooms useful as soaps for washing your hands?

A) Yes    B) No    C) Maybe

**Question 13.29**  Can you wash your hands with kitchen dish soap?

A) Yes    B) No    C) Maybe

**Question 13.30**  Is ammonia a good solution to clean and disinfect surfaces from viruses?

A) Yes    B) No    C) Maybe

**Question 13.31**  Can I use something acidic like vinegar to disinfect my hands?

A) Yes    B) No    C) Maybe

**Question 13.32**  Can I use something natural like lemon juice to disinfect my hands?

A) Yes      B) No      C) Maybe

**Question 13.33**  Can I use a glass cleaner like Windex and feel like I am safe from COVID-19?

A) Yes      B) No      C) Maybe

## Part 5: When to Wash Hands Part 2

This section checks to see if you know when you should wash your hands. Fig. 13.10 shows suds, which are an important way to know that the soap is getting on your hands.

**Fig. 13.10**  Handwashing with lather and running water.

**Question 13.34**  Should you wash your hands before you eat?

A) Yes, always
B) No, never
C) If you live with people
D) If they are visibly dirty

**Question 13.35**  Should you wash your hands if you touch your mouth while cooking?

A) Yes      B) No      C) Maybe

**Question 13.36**  Is a good time to clean your hands when you go in and out of a meeting?

A) Yes      B) No      C) Maybe

**Question 13.37**  Is it useful to clean your hands when going in and out of a building?

A) Yes      B) No      C) Maybe

**Question 13.38** Is it useful to clean your hands after being passed a paper from someone else?

A) Yes     B) No     C) Maybe

**Question 13.39** Will washing your hands only with water kill a virus?

A) Yes     B) No     C) Maybe

**Question 13.40** Will covering your hands with soap but not rinsing kill a virus?

A) Yes     B) No     C) Maybe

**Question 13.41** What are some common ways that people fail to wash their hands correctly? (Select all that apply)

A) They use liquid soap instead of solid soap
B) They use solid soap instead of liquid soap
C) They did not use soap
D) They put soap on without enough water
E) They do not wash long enough
F) They wash too long
G) They contaminate their hands after washing them by touching a door handle
H) They splashed water around onto their clothes
I) They did not rinse their hands
J) They hold their hands down, so water drains from their fingers

**Question 13.42** What are some other common ways that people fail to wash their hands correctly? (Select all that apply)

A) They wash the faucet at the same time
B) They do not wash all the surfaces of their hands
C) They do not rinse their hands
D) They rinse their hands too long
E) They contaminate their hands on an unwashed faucet handle
F) They dry their hands on the inside of their shirt
G) They dry their hands on their trousers

**Answers to Quiz 13**

## Part 1: Mucous Membranes

**Question 13.1: A, Inside of the nose, and B, Inside of the mouth**
*Feedback:* A and B are mucous membranes. C, the skin on the back of the hand is sealed and does not qualify as a mucous membrane.

**Question 13.2: A, Yes**
*Feedback:* Yes, contact lenses will touch your eye (a mucous membrane), so your hands should be clean when you touch the lenses.

**Question 13.3: C, Viruses and bacteria are not visible to the naked eye**
*Feedback:* Viruses and bacteria can be transferred from your hands to your food and infect you when you eat it.

**Question 13.4: A, Yes**
*Feedback:* Yes. Paper cuts are usually deep enough to break through the layers of the skin and count as a break in your skin.

**Question 13.5: A, Yes**
*Feedback:* Yes, you are touching the inside of your mouth when picking your teeth. What is on your hands will be on your teeth, which will be in your mouth. Wash your hands first.

## Part 2: When to wash your hands

**Question 13.6a: A, Yes**
*Feedback:* Yes, the door is likely touched frequently by people passing through, so you will need to wash your hands afterward or use your elbow to open the door.

**Question 13.6b: B, No**
*Feedback:* No, however, you should still be cautious if you are not sure whether someone else has touched the push door.

**Question 13.7: B, No**
*Feedback:* No, you do not need to wash your hands afterward because you are the only one who has touched it. A dry tissue does not disinfect, however.

**Question 13.8: A, Yes**
*Feedback:* Yes, you cannot be sure who has touched the light switch, so you will need to wash your hands afterward.

**Question 13.9: B, No**
*Feedback:* No, you do not need to if only considering COVID-19, but other infectious disease agents may be present on the light switch, which suggests a better practice of washing your hands so you can be certain.

**Question 13.10: A, Yes**
*Feedback:* Yes. It is always a good idea to wash your hands when you come in from outside. It is a useful habit for keeping yourself clean and healthy.

## Part 3: Washing your hands properly

**Question 13.11: A, C, F, B, D, E**
*Feedback:* Wet your hands with clean, running water (warm or cold), turn off the tap, and apply soap. Lather your hands by rubbing them together with the soap. Lather the backs of your hands, between your fingers, and under your nails. Scrub your hands for at least 20 seconds. Need a timer? Hum the "Happy Birthday" song from beginning to end twice. Rinse your hands well under clean, running water. Use a clean towel/paper towel to turn the faucet off after you dry your hands. You can also use the paper towel to open the door.

**Question 13.12: D, 20+ seconds**
*Feedback:* D, 20 or more seconds is key to a thorough cleaning of your hands.

**Question 13.13: B, With a clean paper towel**
*Feedback:* B, a clean paper towel is the best way, but the others are all good ways to dry your hands.

**Question 13.14: A, Yes**
*Feedback:* Yes, so use the paper towel to open the door. If this is not possible, use your foot or elbow.

**Question 13.15: A, Yes**
*Feedback:* Yes. The theory says yes. If you use soap to clean the faucet or door handles, yes, it would be safe to touch them.

**Question 13.16: A, Yes**
*Feedback:* Yes, that could re-contaminate your hands if you do not wash the faucet with soap, so use a paper towel to turn it off or wash it.

**Question 13.17: B, No**
*Feedback:* No, your hands are both clean!

**Question 13.18: A, Yes**
*Feedback:* Yes, that could re-contaminate your hands, so use a paper towel to pick it up.


## Part 4: What soaps are effective for washing hands?

**Question 13.19: A, Yes**
*Feedback:* Yes, sink [A] works. There are two pieces of soap.

**Question 13.20: A, Yes**
*Feedback:* Yes, this liquid soap [B] will work for washing hands because it breaks down oils.

**Question 13.21: A, Yes**
*Feedback:* Yes, this shampoo [C] functions as soap and will break down oils and clean your hands.

**Question 13.22: A, Yes**
*Feedback:* Yes, liquid soap [D] is a soap and will work.

**Question 13.23: B, No**
*Feedback:* No, petroleum jelly (Vaseline) [E] is an oil and does not kill viruses.

**Question 13.24: B, No**
*Feedback:* No, these wipes [F] do not contain soap and will not do the job.

**Question 13.25: A, Yes**
*Feedback:* Yes, you can because while it says it is not soap [G], it acts like a soap.

**Question 13.26: B, No**
*Feedback:* No, cold cream [H] can help remove makeup, but it is not soap and does not kill viruses.

**Question 13.27: A, Yes**
*Feedback:* Yes, but these disinfecting wipes [I] are hard on your hands, so do not use routinely.

**Question 13.28: A, Yes**
*Feedback:* Yes, however they are dispensed, they are soap.

**Question 13.29: A, Yes**
*Feedback:* Yes, kitchen dish soap is a soap.

**Question 13.30: B, No**
*Feedback:* No, ammonia by itself cannot be used to disinfect or kill COVID-19. Also note that household cleaning products have warning labels to alert you to serious health risks if ingested, injected, inhaled, or used on bare skin.

**Question 13.31: B, No**
*Feedback:* No, vinegar may help kill bacteria, but it does not kill viruses.

**Question 13.32: B, No**
*Feedback:* No, lemon juice may help kill bacteria, but it does not kill viruses, particularly the SARS-CoV-2 virus.

**Question 13.33: B, No**
*Feedback:* No, Windex Glass Cleaner does not claim to have any disinfecting properties. It is simply used to remove dirt and streaks from glass surfaces. You should follow up with a disinfectant to ensure that the virus is killed.

## Part 5: When to wash your hands part 2

**Question 13.34: A, Yes, always**
*Feedback:* Yes, always. If you have gone from preparing food directly (without contaminating your hands with raw food) to eating, your hands may be already clean.

**Question 13.35: A, Yes**
*Feedback:* Yes, it is good practice to wash your hands if you touch your mouth while cooking for yourself, and you definitely need to when cooking for other people. This might be a reason why infection spreads easily within a house.

**Question 13.36: A, Yes**
*Feedback:* Yes, it is like when a doctor washes their hands before and after seeing a patient.

**Question 13.37: A, Yes**
*Feedback:* Yes, you may have touched something contaminated, such as an elevator button or door handle.

**Question 13.38: A, Yes**
*Feedback:* Yes, the person may be infectious but not showing any signs.

**Question 13.39: B, No**
*Feedback:* No. Washing just with water may mechanically remove some contaminants, but you should use soap.

**Question 13.40: A, Yes**
*Feedback:* Yes, but then you will have soap on your hands.

**Question 13.41: C, D, E, and G**
*Feedback:* Both liquid and bar soap are good to use so long as you put enough soap on your hands, and they are wet. Once you have soap on your hands, you need to make sure you wash them long enough, rinse them, and avoid recontamination caused by touching unclean objects such as doors or faucet handles. You should not splash water onto your clothes. It is ok, even better, to drain the water from your fingertips.

**Question 13.42: B, C, E, F, G**
*Feedback:* Using extra soap to clean the faucet (alongside your hands) is acceptable. Some people will miss washing spots on their hands. After washing your hands, rinsing them fully is crucial so that the soap can pull the contaminants along with it, and it is better to rinse for too long rather than too short. Try to use a paper towel to shut off the water, so you avoid touching the faucet right after washing, then use a new paper towel for your hands. Drying your hands on items such as your clothing is much less desirable.

# 14

# Washing: Hand and Nail Care

This section briefly covers hand and nail care. For example, how to take care of your hands if you have to wash them often.

## Washing Your Hands Too Much Can Be Harmful to Your Skin

You can wash too much and get cracks in your hands. Fig. 14.1 shows what can happen when you wash your hands too much. Cracks in your hands defeat the protective layer of skin. So, do not wash your hands to that point. Certainly not every ten minutes, but wash when they are contaminated, and when you are likely to touch a mucous membrane.

A way to counteract the effects of washing your hands too often is to use hand lotion when your hands are dry or chapped. You can also wear gloves to help prevent your hands from getting chapped. A good time to moisturize is before going to bed each night.

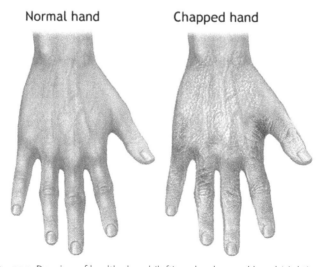

**Fig. 14.1** Drawing of healthy hand (left) and a chapped hand (right).

# Nail Care

To protect your skin, you have to also protect your fingernails and cuticles. These are shown in Fig. 14.2.

To help prevent the spread of germs and nail infections:

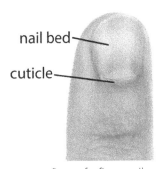

**Fig. 14.2** Parts of a fingernail, including the nail bed and cuticle.

- Keep nails short and trim them often, so they do not puncture your skin. Fauci noted "I clip my nails often because I don't want to carry germs around. If you have long nails, scrape a little soap or sanitizer under the nails." [U14.3]
- Scrub the underside of nails with soap and water (or a nail brush) every time you wash your hands. This removes germs that can fall off into your mouth or eyes.
- Clean any nail grooming tools before use. This keeps them clean from infectious material.
- In commercial settings, such as nail salons, sterilize nail-grooming tools before use.
- Avoid biting or chewing nails or cuticles. This helps keep the skin barrier intact and prevents transferring contamination into your mouth
- Avoid cutting cuticles because they act as barriers to prevent infection.
- Never rip or bite a hangnail. Instead, clip it with a clean, sanitized nail trimmer.

**READ MORE**

[U14.1]  CDC information on hand and finger nail hygiene.
[https://www.cdc.gov/healthywater/hygiene/hand/nail_hygiene.html]

[U14.2]  How to cut fingernail cuticles.
[https://www.youtube.com/watch?v=43YbVhkwiUs]

[U14.3]  Comments from Dr. Fauci about how to avoid getting sick when you're around people all day
[https:// www.washingtonian.com/2016/01/15/how-to-avoid-getting-sick-when-youre-around
-people-all-day/]

# Quiz 14: Hand and Nail Care

Here is a quiz about what are the best practices when it comes to nail care.

**Question 14.1**  Which of the following is the best way to get rid of a hangnail or a pesky cuticle?

A) Bite it off! Tear it off!
B) Emory board
C) Clean, sanitized nail trimmer

**Question 14.2**  When is a good time to moisturize your hands? (Select all that apply)

A) Before washing them
B) After washing them
C) When they are chapped
D) Before going to bed each night

. . . . . . . . . . . . . . . . . . . . . . . . . . . . . . . . . . . . . . . . . . . . . . . . . . . . . . . . . . . . .

**Answers to Quiz 14**

**Question 14.1: C, Clean, sanitized nail trimmer**
*Feedback:* C, using a clean, sanitized nail trimmer is best because you want to avoid contact with your mucous membranes with your hands, and you will be more precise.

**Question 14.2: B, After washing them, C, When they are chapped, and D, Before going to bed each night.**
*Feedback:* All are good times except for A. Putting on moisturizer and then washing your hands just wastes moisturizer.

# 15
# Washing: Hand Sanitizer

## Use of Hand Sanitizer

Washing with soap and water is preferred to using hand sanitizer, especially for removing dirt. Washing with soap and water also removes a broader variety of microbes. Used correctly, hand sanitizers can kill coronavirus while offering portability (Fig. 15.1). In some cases, hand sanitizers also offer skin conditioning that helps seal skin cracks from microbes.

**Fig. 15.1** Woman with a face mask using hand sanitizer.

**READ MORE**

[U15.1]    Search "Hand sanitizer"

## Theory of Hand Sanitizer

Hand Sanitizer is an effective alternative to handwashing when handwashing is not practical, for example, while traveling. Alcohols destroy pathogens by breaking their cells and destroying viral proteins. This disinfects your hand when used correctly. You need to use enough, as Fig. 15.2 shows.

Hand sanitizers do not remove dirt, oil, or debris. Visibly soiled or oily hands should not be sterilized or cleaned with hand sanitizer use alone. Handwashing is superior to hand sanitizer with visibly soiled hands.

The effective or active ingredient in hand sanitizer is usually ethanol, propanol, or isopropyl alcohol, or benzalkonium chloride (which is less accepted). Other chemicals can also be used. Most hand sanitizers, particularly those using propanol and isopropyl alcohol, are UNSAFE to ingest (drink or put on food). Doing so can cause blindness and injury to your kidneys.

**Fig. 15.2** Use a large dollop of hand sanitizer to disinfect properly.

The CDC and FDA recommend that hand sanitizers have at least 60% ethanol or 70% isopropanol alcohol [U15.3]. During a shortage of hand sanitizer, ethanol (alcohol used for drinking) can be used for hand sterilization. The alcohol must be at least 120 proof (60% alcohol content). There are hand sanitizer recipes on the Internet for making sanitizer that is more comfortable to use and less harsh on your hands.

If you keep a bottle in your car, this can serve as back up when you go out in case you forget the one you travel with. It also serves as a visual reminder to sanitize when you get in and out of your car.

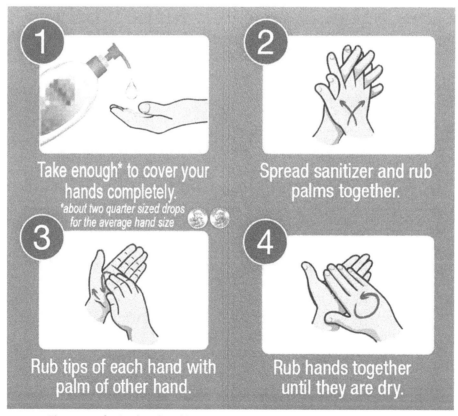

1 Take enough* to cover your hands completely.
*about two quarter sized drops for the average hand size

2 Spread sanitizer and rub palms together.

3 Rub tips of each hand with palm of other hand.

4 Rub hands together until they are dry.

**Fig. 15.3** The steps of using hand sanitizer.

To make sanitizer easier to use, you might wish to keep a travel bottle next to your keys and mask. To make it fun or more pleasant, you can add a drop of flavoring or essential oil to the less good-smelling ones, but be mindful that good-smelling sanitizers might lead to children wanting to drink them.

## How to Use Hand Sanitizer

When using hand sanitizer, use enough product to cover all surfaces of your hands completely. This will often be more than one pump. Your entire hands should be wet. Then rub your hands together for at least 20 seconds until your hands are dry. Make sure to saturate and cover your hands thoroughly. Fig. 15.3 shows this diagrammatically.

**LEARN MORE**

**[U15.2]**  Dr. John Campbell showing how to use hand sanitizer
[https://www.youtube.com/watch?v=MH3ogesiTiY]

**[U15.3]**  CDC on hand sanitizers
[https://www.cdc.gov/coronavirus/2019-ncov/hcp/hand-hygiene.html]

# Quiz 15: Hand Sanitizer Use and Safety

This quiz is about hand sanitizer ingredients, safety, and how to use it properly.

**Question 15.1**   Can you make sanitizer using beer for the alcohol?
A) Yes        B) No        C) Maybe

**Question 15.2**   Can I use antifreeze to sterilize my hands?
A) Yes        B) No        C) Maybe

**Question 15.3**   Are liquid hand sanitizers safe to drink?
A) Yes        B) No        C) Maybe

**Question 15.4**   Should you use a hairdryer to kill the virus on your skin or in your nostrils?
A) Yes        B) No        C) Maybe

**Question 15.5**   Should you use hand sanitizer in your house?
A) Yes        B) No        C) Maybe

**Question 15.6**   In a meeting, someone asks you to pass a phone to them. Should you use hand sanitizer then?
A) Yes        B) No        C) Maybe

**Question 15.7**   Should you use hand sanitizer after going into the grocery store and after wiping the handle of the shopping cart with a disinfecting wipe?
A) Yes        B) No        C) Maybe

**Question 15.8**   Should you use hand sanitizer after coming into your apartment building, having gone through a series of doors, and pushing an elevator button?
A) Yes        B) No        C) Maybe

**Question 15.9**   Should you use hand sanitizer after touching a turnstile in a subway?
A) Yes        B) No        C) Maybe

**Question 15.10**   Should you use hand sanitizer after touching money?
A) Yes        B) No        C) Maybe

**Question 15.11**   If your hands are visibly soiled, should you use hand sanitizer?
A) Yes        B) No        C) Maybe

**Question 15.12**  How much hand sanitizer should you use to sanitize your hands?

A) A teaspoon
B) Two quarters
C) A drop
D) One-half pump

**Answers to Quiz 15**

**Question 15.1: B, No**
*Feedback:* No, beer does not have enough alcohol to kill infectious agents.

**Question 15.2: B, No**
*Feedback:* No, antifreeze does not contain the right kind of alcohol to kill infectious agents, and can be lethal if ingested.

**Question 15.3: B, No**
*Feedback:* No, drinking many hand sanitizers can cause blindness and kidney failure; some are other types of poison.

**Question 15.4: B, No**
*Feedback:* No, a hairdryer will burn you before it kills the virus.

**Question 15.5: B, No, or C, Maybe**
*Feedback:* No/maybe. You do not generally need to because you are better off with soap and water, but if you cannot easily get to soap and water, use hand sanitizer.

**Question 15.6: A, Yes**
*Feedback:* Yes. Particularly if you are at risk of touching your face.

**Question 15.7: B, No**
*Feedback:* No, the wipe will have cleaned that surface.

**Question 15.8: B, No**
*Feedback:* No, you can use soap and water when you get inside your apartment, but make sure not to touch your face before you get to wash your hands.

**Question 15.9: A, Yes**
*Feedback:* Yes. Particularly if you are at risk of touching your face.

**Question 15.10: A, Yes**
*Feedback:* Yes. It is a great idea in case you end up touching your face.

**Question 15.11: B, No**
*Feedback:* No, hand sanitizer is not effective at removing debris or oil. Wash hands with soap and water when soiled.

**Question 15.12: A, A teaspoon, or B, Two quarters**
*Feedback:* A teaspoon or two quarters worth will do a regular-sized hand. A drop is too little, and one-half pump depends on your dispenser, but often is not enough.

# 16

# Washing: Do not Touch Your Face or Mucous Membranes!

## Do not Touch Your Face

Touching an infectious person or surface that has a virus on it and then touching your face (especially your eyes, nose, or mouth) is a way for viruses and germs to invade your body and make you sick.

Look, you are going to touch your face. We all do, as Fig. 16.1 and 16.2 illustrate. We stroke our hair, we scratch our nose, we remove a speck from our eyes. We might do it naturally over 20 times an hour. You will need to practice to stop.

The effect of touching your face when you have a virus or bacteria on your hands can put you at risk for infection. To understand the effect of touching your face with a pathogen, imagine you have just worked with hot peppers and scratch your eye. You will not do that again! If you have touched a surface that has a virus on it and then touched a mucous membrane on your face, you can infect yourself.

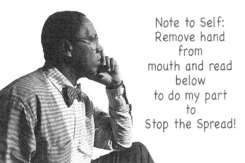

Note to Self:
Remove hand from
mouth and read
below
to do my part
to
Stop the Spread!

**Fig. 16.1** You should avoid touching your face, even when thinking about the concept.

**Fig. 16.2** There are many ways to touch your face; you should do none of them.

## Game: How Many Times Do You Touch Your Face and Head?

To not touch your face, you have to relearn a reflex. A way to do this is to play a game with someone else watching you, or record and score yourself. You get one point each time the other person touches their face. Set a time limit, like five or ten minutes.

If someone touches their face, you can yell, "face!" This approach is also used when teaching public speaking to decrease the frequency of saying "um." You can also use a clicker to note each time when this happens.

This game is used to train workers in some restaurants. You can also get your children and friends to play the "do not touch your face" game. Reward them if they catch you doing it.

It is not easy, but over time you will get better. And getting better helps, even if you are not perfect, you can reduce the amount and frequency that you might infect yourself. The remainder of this section has strategies to help you win this game.

**LEARN MORE**

There are example videos that you can also use on our associated website, and many videos online would work too.

**[U16.1]**  Scrubs video
[https://www.youtube.com/watch?v=vakZhVMsM-4]

**[U16.2]**  News clips including people touching their face
[https://www.youtube.com/watch?v=mA1wqjaeKj0]

**[U16.3]**  President Reagan talking and sometimes touching his face
[https://www.youtube.com/watch?v=Pgs-LaWyUJI]

## Strategies for Touching Your Face Less: Reminders

We know that COVID-19 can be spread by people coming into contact with the virus and then touching their eyes, nose, and mouth. Once you become aware of this, you can try to stop touching your face, but it can be quite challenging to overcome. Why? Researchers have found that people touch their face subconsciously (we do not even realize we are doing it), and it can be a part of a self-soothing mechanism.

Not touching your face helping stop the spread, but is difficult to do. The first step is to raise your own awareness, which you have started to do just by reading this paragraph, so keep reading below for several tips. Not touching your face is far more important when outside of your house.

What action can you take to be mindful of touching your face? Remind yourself with a visual or sensory action.

Example Actions:

- Put a Post-It note on your computer (Fig. 16.3).

- Add an image to your phone's home screen background to remind yourself to stop touching your face.

- Tie a string around your finger as a reminder to not touch your face.

**Fig. 16.3** You can use a Post-it note to remember not to touch your face.

## Strategies for Touching Your Face Less: Barriers

Another strategy for touching your face less is to create a barrier for your hands to never reach your face by putting something between your hands and face, like a facemask or glasses (Fig. 16.4). Putting a facemask and glasses together would also be a great idea because facemasks worn without glasses leave your eyes vulnerable, and glasses without a facemask miss covering your nostrils and mouth. Wearing both facemask and glasses give you better overall protection. Example actions:

- Hold a clean tissue, chopstick, or pencil to scratch or touch your face.

- Wear a veil or beekeeper hat or a face shield.

- Do not have a mask? Get creative, try to make something with items you have at home. Try a bandana or a motorcycle helmet.

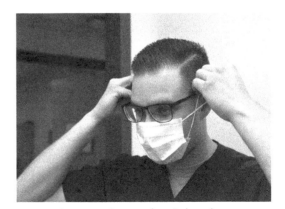

**Fig. 16.4** A man putting on a hospital mask.

# Strategies for Touching Your Face Less: Substitute Behaviors

You can also substitute other behaviors for touching your face. Replace the behavior that can be a pathway for infection into your body with something that does not have you touching your face. Giving your hands something else to do can help from subconsciously touching your face. Below are some examples of actions you can try.

Example actions:

- Tap your chest or rub your arm
- Squeeze a stress ball or spin a fidget spinner (Fig. 16.5)

What should you do if you have to touch your face?

If you have to touch your face, washing your hands and cleaning surfaces before touching your face is ideal. So, if, for instance, you have to take a pair of contacts out, just take a moment to wash your hands with soap and water before, and it can help you from becoming infected if you happen to have something on your hands.

**Fig. 16.5** A fidget spinner can help distract you from touching your face.

**READ MORE**

[U16.4]  Avoid touching your face to reduce risk
[https://www.northeastern.edu/covid-19-how-to-be-safe-and-resilient/#/lessons/LoRf7h2BLz_5i87W498XANlxuI2Qd87H]

[U16.5]  How to touch your face less
[https://theoatmeal.com/comics/touch_face]

## Quiz 16: Washing Hands and Touching Your Face

This quiz checks to see if you know when you should wash your hands. We include this quiz here because of the importance of the topic, giving additional practice.

**Question 16.1**    Is it safe to facepalm anymore if your face is clean AND you first wash your hands?

A) Yes    B) No    C) Maybe

**Question 16.2**    Should you wash your hands before eating?

A) Yes    B) No    C) Depends

**Question 16.3**    Should you wash your hands after sanitizing them with hand sanitizer?

A) Yes    B) No    C) Only if they are physically dirty

**Question 16.4**    Should you wash your hands after working with surface sanitizer or disinfectant?

A) Yes    B) No    C) Depends

**Question 16.5**    If a grocery store clerk hands you a receipt, should you clean your hands?

A) Yes    B) No    C) Maybe

**Question 16.6**    Can you touch your eyes, nose, and mouth mucous membrane with clean hands?

A) Yes    B) No    C) Depends

**Question 16.7**    Should you touch your mucous membranes after picking something up from the floor?

A) Yes    B) No    C) Maybe

**Question 16.8**    Can you scratch your face with a clean tissue?

A) Yes    B) No    C) Maybe

**Question 16.9**    Can playing with a pen help you not touch your face?

A) Yes    B) No    C) Maybe

**Question 16.10**  Which are useful strategies to substitute for touching your eyes, nose, and mouth? (Choose all that apply)

A) Eating snacks
B) Playing with a Rubik's cube
C) Walking the dog
D) Picking your nose
E) Picking your teeth
F) Scratching your head
G) Drumming your fingers
H) Picking your fingers
I) Filing your nails
J) Squeezing a ball

**Question 16.11**  Would wearing a bracelet that jingles be a good strategy to help you touch your face less?

A) Yes      B) No      C) Maybe

## Answers to Quiz 16

**Question 16.1: A, Yes**
*Feedback:* Yes, it is safe to face palm as long as you wash your hands first.

**Question 16.2: A, Yes**
*Feedback:* Yes. If you are eating alone, quarantined and isolated, and washed your hands while preparing food, no, you do not necessarily have to, but it is good practice to wash your hands. If you are eating with others and going to pass food with your hands and they have touched your mouth, your hands can be infectious. Hands that have touched the mouth is a major transmission method between people in families.

**Question 16.3: C, Only if they are physically dirty**
*Feedback:* C, only if your hands are physically dirty, as soap and water will do additional cleaning on your hands.

**Question 16.4: C, Depends**
*Feedback:* It depends. Do you need to disinfect your hands? No, they are already disinfected by the surface sanitizer or disinfectant. But, if the surface sanitizer is harsh, you may wish to wash your hands afterward because the chemicals may hurt your hands, or you can wear gloves to prevent the harsh chemicals from touching your hands. Most surface sanitizers are harsh on your hands.

**Question 16.5: A, Yes**
*Feedback:* Yes. The only exception would be if the clerk who handed the receipt to you just washed their hands and did not handle anything else, or you took it directly from the machine. You might reasonably wait until you are outside the store to sanitize if you have to touch further things.

**Question 16.6: A, Yes**
*Feedback:* Yes. After you have cleaned your hands is the best time to touch your face!

**Question 16.7: B, No**
*Feedback:* No. Touching objects on the floor may have infectious material on them. Wash your hands before touching your face.

**Question 16.8: A, Yes**
*Feedback:* Yes, a fresh tissue will be clean.

**Question 16.9: A, Yes**
*Feedback:* Yes, a pen can help distract you from touching your face.

**Question 16.10: B, C, G, I, J**
*Feedback:* Useful strategies will keep your hands away from your face and occupied, so you do not inadvertently touch your face.

**Question 16.11: A, Yes**
*Feedback:* Yes. A jangling bracelet would remind you when you move your hands. But, you have to wash and dry it with your hands as it can become contaminated as it is on your hands.

# 17

# Washing: Objects and Surfaces

The coronavirus is believed to be most commonly transmitted by droplets. These droplets can and will land on surfaces and require cleaning and disinfectant to decrease disease transmission through surfaces. The current evidence suggests that coronavirus may be viable for hours to days on some surfaces.

The CDC currently recommends the cleaning of surfaces that appear visibly soiled (e.g., in Fig. 17.1) and then disinfecting those surfaces. Cleaning is even more important in locations and homes with suspected or confirmed COVID-19.

**Fig. 17.1** Wash children's toys frequently.

**READ MORE**

[U17.1]   COVID-19: How long does the coronavirus last on surfaces? [https://www.bbc.com/future/article/20200317-covid-19-how-long-does-the-coronavirus-last-on-surfaces]

## Cleaning vs. Disinfecting

Cleaning is the removal of dirt, grease, oil, and impurities from surfaces. Cleaning can physically remove bacteria and viruses but does not destroy them. Cleaning does decrease the amount and risk of disease or infection, as Fig. 17.2 notes.

Disinfecting is the use of chemicals, heat, or UV light to destroy bacteria and viruses on a surface. Disinfecting is most effective after an object has been cleaned.

**Fig. 17.2** How to clean to avoid the COVID-19 virus (CDC poster).

## What Are Commonly Touched (High-Touch) Surfaces?

What are commonly touched surfaces? In work environments, they are surfaces that multiple people touch. The underneath side of a table is probably not a high-touch surface. Door handles, handrails, and elevator buttons are high-touch surfaces. These all should be cleaned at least daily if multiple people are working there.

This list includes floors inside your home and work (because of shoes), refrigerator door handles (particularly outside your home), and light switches. These all should be cleaned at least daily if people are entering and leaving your home.

**Fig. 17.3** High-touch items to clean and to clean your hands after touching: keys, gas pump nozzles and keypad, and money.

Disinfecting these surfaces can have multiple payoffs. Each person that is not infected also means that people that they would infect are also not infected. Fig. 17.3 shows several examples.

Here is a longer list. You can modify it to suit your circumstances:

- Refrigerator handles
- Light switches
- Microwave buttons and handles
- Front door inside doorknob
- Garage door inside doorknob
- Refrigerator door handle
- Microwave handle/buttons
- TV Remote control
- Living Room coffee table
- Living room, kitchen, and garage entry light switches
- Keyboards and mouse on shared computers
- Reusable water bottles that travel in/out of the home
- Outside of hand-sanitizer bottles that travel in/out of the home

## How to Clean Surfaces

Here is how to clean and disinfect hard surfaces:

1. Disposable gloves should be worn if available.
2. Surfaces that are visibly soiled should be cleaned with soap and water.
3. The surface should then be disinfected.
   a. CDC recommends using an EPA-registered household disinfectant (follow manufacturer's directions), such as a disinfecting wipe, or

b. A solution containing at least 60% (ethanol) alcohol by concentration, or
c. Dilute household bleach solution.
    5 tablespoons of bleach per gallon of water, or
    4 teaspoons bleach per quart of water or
    20 ml of bleach with 1 litre of water

## How to Clean Clothes and Linens

CDC recommends washing clothes and linens according to the manufacturer's recommendations. If there is suspected contamination with coronavirus or other contagions, you should use gloves when handling soiled items and wash hands immediately following.

Some shoes may be hard to clean or cannot be put through a washing machine. You should consider leaving shoes at the door. Many cultures and households already do this, but it may be worth incorporating into your house now if you are not doing it already.

# Quiz 17: Cleaning Objects and More

Here is a quiz on cleaning items you often touch, such as cell phones, keys, credit cards, cash, gas pumps, and ATM keypads.

## Part 1: Cleaning Objects

**Question 17.1**   If you went through this door, should you wash your hands afterward?

A) Yes     B) No     C) Maybe

**Question 17.2**   Should you wash your hands after playing chess?

A) Yes     B) No     C) Maybe

**Question 17.3**   Is it safe to eat veggies rinsed just with tap water?

A) Yes     B) No     C) Maybe

**Question 17.4**  For each item below, does it need to be cleaned before use? (Yes/No)

| | |
|---|---|
| _____ Tissues | _____ Car keys |
| _____ Phones | _____ Door handles |
| _____ Toothbrushes | _____ Food from inside a car |
| _____ Gas station pumps | _____ Hands |
| _____ Shopping carts | _____ A garbage can in your garage |
| _____ Television remote | _____ Fresh produce |

## Part 2: How to Clean a Surface

This quiz will help you decide if you can recognize making smart choices when it comes to cleaning surfaces.

**Question 17.5**  Do you need to clean a toy or pacifier dropped on the floor of a train?

A) Yes     B) No     C) Maybe

**Question 17.6**  Can you use the "five-second rule" if your baby's pacifier is dropped on a freshly swept public floor?

A) Yes     B) No     C) Maybe

**Question 17.7**  Can a child play with a toy wiped down with a sanitizing wipe that was then air-dried?

A) Yes     B) No     C) Maybe

**Question 17.8**  Can a cell phone and earbuds, wiped down with 60–90% ethanol alcohol on a paper towel, be considered safe from the virus?

A) Yes  B) No  C) Maybe

**Question 17.9**  Can you feel safe with a stuffed animal put through the washer and allowed to air dry?

A) Yes  B) No  C) Maybe

**Question 17.10**  Can the virus live on a stuffed animal left to sit in sunlight for a week?

A) Yes  B) No  C) Maybe

**Question 17.11**  Is freshly washed laundry with sensitive skin detergent considered COVID-19 free?

A) Yes  B) No  C) Maybe

**Question 17.12**  Is a doorknob wiped with detergent and sprayed with sanitizer free of the virus?

A) Yes  B) No  C) Maybe

**Answers to Quiz 17**

## Part 1: Cleaning Objects

**Question 17.1: A, Yes**
*Feedback:* Yes, if you touched the keypad. No, if it was unlocked and you used your elbow or if it is in your own house.

**Question 17.2: A, Yes**
*Feedback:* Yes, another person has recently touched what you have touched.

**Question 17.3: A, Yes**
*Feedback:* Yes, at this time, the FDA recommends only washing your fruits and vegetables with cool running water. They have not found any evidence of people getting COVID-19 from eating food.

**Question 17.4: No, Yes, Yes, Yes, No, No, Yes, Yes, Yes, No, Yes, Yes**
Tissues: No, they are already clean.
Car keys: Yes, because they are often touched by hands that are often dirty.
Phones: Yes, because they go in your pocket or are placed on surfaces outside your home.
Door handles: Yes, because multiple people touch them.
Toothbrush: No, it gets cleaned after each use, and your hands were cleaned before brushing your teeth; we hope.
Food from inside a can: No, it was cleaned prior to being put into the can.
Gas station pump: Yes, but clean your hands after use as well.
Hands: Yes, particularly if eating or drinking.
Shopping Carts: Yes, or also clean your hands after use.
The garbage can in your garage: No, but wash your hands after pulling the garbage cans in or out.
Television remote: Yes, people touch the TV remote frequently, and you should be sure to wash your hands afterward.
Fresh produce: Yes, but only rinse your fruits and veggies with water. You do not need to use soap or other chemicals as these can make you sick.

## Part 2: How to clean a surface

**Question 17.5: A, Yes**
*Feedback:* Yes, items that go into someone's mouth or might touch someone's face need to be cleaned.

**Question 17.6: B, No**
*Feedback:* No, because the pacifier has not been cleaned or sanitized.

**Question 17.7: A, Yes**
*Feedback:* Yes, a toy wiped down with disinfecting wipes is fine.

**Question 17.8: A, Yes**
*Feedback:* Yes, ethanol alcohol at 60–95% kills the virus, isopropyl alcohol at 70–95%.

**Question 17.9: A, Yes**

*Feedback:* Yes, as long as you wash the stuffed animal with soap or detergent, washing will kill the virus.

**Question 17.10: B, No**

*Feedback:* No, the COVID-19 virus cannot last a week on any surface at room temperature, so it can be considered safe.

**Question 17.11: A, Yes**

*Feedback:* Yes, any detergent will kill the virus, and the heat of the dryer will also help.

**Question 17.12: A, Yes**

*Feedback:* Yes, as long as nobody has touched the doorknob after it has been cleaned before you touched it.

# 18

# Looking After Yourself with the Added Benefits to Your Immune System

Looking after yourself, or self-care, supports your overall health and also benefits your immune system. Self-care helps you to be your best, both physically and mentally. It helps you deal with stress more effectively, such as from the pandemic. Self-care actions such as balanced nourishment, rest, and exercise additionally benefit your immune system. A strong immune system is a way to obstruct pandemics, as shown in Fig. 2.2 (also on the back cover) and 3.1, and is your last line of defense.

This section covers the need to look after yourself (Fig. 18.1) and ways to do that during the pandemic. This section starts with awareness of your emotions and your situation in general and then moves into practical ways (skills) to improve your mental balance, health, and immune system. There are resources and a quiz to give you opportunities to help you conceptualize these practices and then incorporating them into your life.

**Fig. 18.1** There are numerous ways you can provide self-care.

# Awareness

Going through a pandemic can stir up all sorts of feelings. Our ordinary lives have been disrupted. The absence of routine and limited social interactions can be taxing on our mental health. News cycles are available day and night and are competing to get your attention. Sometimes, to pull you in, organizations sensationalize titles or news as click bait, all of which can cause distress.

Everyone is being impacted negatively by the pandemic in one way or another. Strong emotions can come from worrying about exposing yourself or family members to the virus. Some people still need to go to work and are vulnerable to infection. That can be scary. Other people have been laid off, which can be another large source of uneasiness because they do not know how they will pay for essentials. Then some individuals are working remotely and trying to maintain their productivity or job, which can be challenging in their home environment. Fear and anxiety are normal responses to uncertain situations. It is good to understand how varying levels of worry or concern affect us.

High levels of stress can negatively affect our mental and physical health. It can make us feel overwhelmed, which can cause us to shut down physically (increase fatigue, lower immune functioning), mentally (increase depression, lower concentration), and behaviorally (lower vigilance around safety, lower motivation to keep up safe practices).

**Fig. 18.2** You should take time for awareness; it can reduce stress.

Having some stress can be helpful; it allows us to be aware of danger and may prevent us from putting ourselves into unsafe situations. For instance, during the pandemic, stress can be the motivator to help us shelter in place or wear a mask in public.

Taking some time to be aware (Fig. 18.2) and to maintain your emotional health can help give you the ability to navigate and regulate your emotions. For example, practicing gratitude can help shift your thoughts from "I am stuck at home" to "I am safe at home," which can change your perspective and emotions. There are more tips and information on the Internet and later

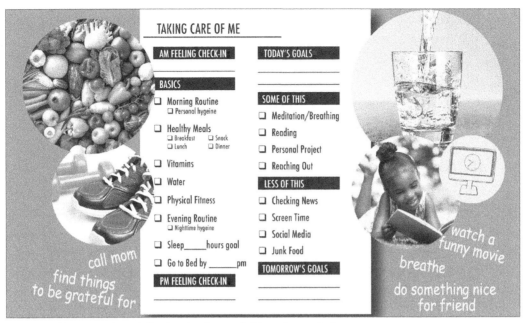

**Fig. 18.3** Taking care of me daily planning list, available as Appendix 2.

in this section on coping skills based on being conscious of emotions and responding in an effective way to challenging situations.

## Planning and Creating Structure to Your Day

Plan your day with awareness to protect your emotional health. Routines can give us the ability to actively promote positive psychological health activities and habits into our day and thoughts. Planning your day using a list like the one shown in Fig. 18.3 can offer a level of fortification that makes it easier to catch spiraling negative thoughts and feelings. This extra planning can also help you get sufficient sleep, which, as research has shown numerous times, can help your immune system. If planning causes you stress, then reach out to people around you or professionals for help.

The need for routine and structure in our everyday lives has never been more important than during this pandemic. Sheltering in place, quarantining, and self-isolating due to the pandemic has disrupted our routine. Routines are known to make people more productive, happier, and healthier. It is also a way of maintaining a level of normalcy for yourself and your family during uncertain times, which reduces stress. Routines can also push you to maintain healthy habits such as exercising, eating proper meals, and sleeping on a schedule, which also benefits your mental wellbeing. When planning your day, take some time to engage in activities you enjoy. That could be praying or meditating, or it might be listening to music, reading a book, or creating art.

**READ MORE**

**[U18.1]**   Downloadable checklist as PDF
[http://StopTheSpread.health/takingcareofme2.pdf] and as Appendix 2

# Computer Time, News, and Social Media

It is useful to stay informed about the news, and you may keep connected via social media, but do not watch, read, listen to, or surf the Internet all the time. You must be mindful of the trade-offs between how much value you get from the news and the emotional impact it has on you. A method to decrease mental exhaustion from the news is to pick a couple of news sources you trust and then pick just a couple of times a day to stay up-to-date. You can set a timer to make sure you do not get sucked in. For an extreme example, see Fig. 18.4. Too much information can overload your mind.

**Fig. 18.4** You might wish to budget your screen time.

Also, be mindful of the amount of time you spend on screens, particularly at night. Blue light at night can make it harder to fall asleep. You can either mindfully avoid screens two to three hours before bed or wear glasses that block blue light while on your laptop or watching television. You can also consider finding and using apps for your phone, laptop, and tablets to reduce blue light from the display in the evening.

When choosing a resource for news, be aware of how you feel when you are getting the information. If you are always feeling overwhelmed by a specific channel, try another source and see if that helps. It is okay to take a break or distance yourself from the news for a few days if you feel overwhelmed.

It is also important to keep in mind that the mainstream news media is a business, and they focus on news stories that grab people's attention. The stories go one step further and sensationalize the news to draw more people in while some small stories get overlooked. News sources like the website "Not all News is Bad," and some good news channels on YouTube, focus on small but positive news happening around the world and may help you remember that even during this pandemic, good things are still happening. If you do not have a news source you trust about the pandemic, we recommend Dr. John Campbell's daily YouTube videos as a great source for information on the pandemic. His information is well researched and explained (he is a retired nursing professor).

**READ MORE**

[U18.2]    Harvard Health Letter on blue light and sleep
[https://www.health.harvard.edu/staying-healthy/blue-light-has-a-dark-side]

**LEARN MORE**

[U18.3]    Search: "Blue light filter for screens"

[U18.4]    Dr. John Campbell's YouTube channel provides balanced news about COVID-19
[https://www.youtube.com/user/Campbellteaching]

## Focus on Physiological Health to Build Mental Strength

Emotional wellbeing is connected to physical health. Maslow's Hierarchy of Needs (Fig. 18.5) can help visualize the connection between the two. At the bottom of the pyramid are basic physical needs like breathing, eating, and sleeping. When you first focus on your basic physical needs, you will have a

**Fig. 18.5** Maslow's Hierarchy of Needs.

solid foundation to work on the higher sections of the pyramid. Think about the beginning of the pandemic; people focused on the basics like getting to the grocery store to get food, water, and toilet paper. The higher levels of the pyramid, like self-actualization, are harder to work on when we do not have our basic needs met. Self-actualization is a person's desire to aim for their full potential. Working on higher levels is easier when the lower levels are maintained. Thinking of Maslow's Hierarchy as a tool to help you take a step back and examine what is most important for you to be working on can help your emotional wellbeing.

**LEARN MORE**

**[U18.5]**    Explanation of Maslow's Hierarchy of Needs
[https://www.youtube.com/watch?v=L0PKWTta7lU]

# Breathing

Breathing is a bodily function that we do not often think about. However, it is well known that stress can lead to anxiety, which can lead to shallow breathing and shortness of breath. The lack of proper breathing can zap your energy and motivation, which can lead to further anxiety.

Combat this negative cycle by checking in on your breath, as suggested by Fig. 18.6. If you find that you notice yourself holding your breath or unable to take a nice deep breath, try a mindful breathing exercise. There are many breathing exercises available. Breathing exercises have a calming effect and can restore your breath to a natural rhythm, and people have been known to use them to help fall asleep faster. An example of a breathing exercise is the 4-7-8 exercise.

**Fig. 18.6** Paced Breathing can help reduce stress.

Try the 4-7-8 Breathing Exercise explained in Fig. 18.7, and see if it affects your pulse. Before you begin, find your heart rate. If you do not have a fitness watch or other device to take your pulse, it is easy to find your heart rate with your index and middle fingers. Do not use your thumb because its pulse can be felt as well. Make sure you are sitting or lying down with your legs uncrossed. Standing can increase your heart rate. Exercise can also increase your heart rate, so it is best to take your pulse either before

**Breathe More. Stress Less.**

Use the 4-7-8 breathing technique to lower your stress level

Close your mouth and breathe in through your nose for a silent count of 4

Hold your breath for a silent count of 7

Exhale through your mouth for a silent count of 8

Repeat the cycle 3 more times for a total of 4 breaths

**Fig. 18.7** The 4, 7, 8 breathing technique can help reduce stress.

you exercise or after you finished exercising and cooled down. Place your index and middle finger either on the underside of your wrist, the base of the thumb, or the hollow of your neck to the side of your windpipe. Slowly move your fingers until you feel the thump of your pulse. Once you find it, count the number of beats in 15 seconds and then multiply that number by 4 to find your beats per minute. Remember that number.

Now, try the 4-7-8 breathing exercise. Breathe in for four seconds, hold that breath for seven seconds, and then slowly release for eight seconds. Repeat this sequence three times. You may wish to adjust these numbers to suit yourself.

Now take your pulse again the same way as described above and see if you lowered your pulse. Keep in mind that many factors can influence your heart rate.

**READ MORE**

[U18.6]  Target heart rates by age
[https://www.heart.org/en/healthy-living/fitness/fitness-basics/target-heart-rates]

# Eating Well and Staying Hydrated

A balanced diet with nutrient-rich foods and keeping well hydrated helps maintain health and normal body functioning. Fig. 18.8 shows an example. Good nutritional practices are also known to protect your mental wellbeing. It is important to be aware that when stressed, people may not make the best choices when it comes to food. Some people crave junk food and snack mindlessly, while others may overeat or even skip meals altogether. Having this knowledge and planning ways to support healthy choices can safeguard your overall physical and mental health. Try to eat at regular times and opt for healthy choices. Poor eating choices can make you feel guilty later or lead to feelings of sluggishness. In the long term, it can lead to obesity.

**Fig. 18.8** Healthy foods help your immune system.

Nutrient deficiencies can impact your body and our immune system. There is some evidence that Vitamin D deficiency weakens your immune system. Having enough trace metals like zinc can also be important for a robust immune system. Dr. John Campbell notes that some studies show that a significant portion of people have a vitamin D deficiency. If you are at particular risk, you should consult your health care provider about these supplements.

Staying hydrated is also important for good health. It means that you drink enough water. You can tell if you are drinking enough water by your urine color. If it is a pale yellow, straw-colored (light yellow), or lighter, you are hydrated. If your urine is darker (dark yellow, orange, tea-colored), you are dehydrated and should drink more water.

**READ MORE**

[U18.7]  The role of nutrition and health
[https://www.cdc.gov/nccdphp/dnpao/features/national-nutrition-month/index.html]

**LEARN MORE**

[U18.8]  Dr. John Campbell on vitamin D (short 21:40 min.)
[https://www.youtube.com/watch?v=Bga_qG30JyY]

[U18.9]  Dr. John Campbell on vitamin D (longer 32 min.)
[https://www.youtube.com/watch?v=_fIMkigtnk4L]

[U18.10]  Can dietary supplements boost your immunity?
[https://news.psu.edu/video/618504/2020/05/04/research/can-supplements-boost-my-immunity
-ask-cidd]

# Sleep

Protect your sleep. Good quality sleep has restorative powers for your body as shown in Fig. 18.9. It supports your immune system, brain function, and helps you to manage stress and depression better. To protect your sleep, create a calming bedroom environment. The use of dimmable lights and comfortable bedding are ways to create a good sleep environment. There is a lot more information online if this remains a problem. Another tip: if you have a hard time falling asleep because you tend to let worries float around in your head, try writing your thoughts down, and let them go before you to drift off. An Internet search will help you find more information and tips.

**Fig. 18.9** Sleep helps reduce stress and helps your immune system.

Most people have fairly consistent sleep and wake schedules during their early childhood, but are much less consistent now. Sometimes this is due to work or life constraints, but if you can manage it, the best tip for good sleep is to set regular sleep and wake times and follow them. No matter what age you are, a stable sleep-wake cycle will help you wake feeling more rested and fall asleep easier.

**READ MORE**

[U18.11]  Mayo Clinic's notes on how to sleep
[https://www.mayoclinic.org/healthy-lifestyle/adult-health/in-depth/sleep/art-20048379]

[U18.12]  Search: "How to sleep better"

# Physical Fitness

There is a strong connection between physical health and psychological health. The benefits of physical fitness cannot be left out of this discussion. Exercise gives you time to unwind and not think or talk about the pandemic.

Go for a walk or exercise at home with an online workout. If you are new to exercise and do not know what to do, there are plenty of guides for simple workouts available online. Regular exercise at least 1-2 hours before bed has been proven to reduce stress and anxiety and improve sleep. Check with your healthcare provider on how to start exercising, especially if you

Fig. 18.10 Yoga and pets can help reduce stress.

have any medical concerns or have not exercised much in the past. You can start small. Even a quick 5-minute exercise can boost your spirits (walking counts). You can add a minute per day or per week to improve your stamina and motivation and make it a habit. Fig. 18.10 illustrates that yoga can be helpful, as well.

## Social Connections

In a time where social distancing is the new normal, it is important to realize that social distancing means *physically* distancing yourself from others to stop the spread. It does not mean we should stop socializing and connecting with others. Just keep yourself at least six feet apart from others. Socializing is hugely important to your spirit. Connecting with others can release serotonin, the "feel-good hormone," that can help alleviate stress.

There are many options to connect creatively with others while still maintaining physical distance. Computer- and phone-based systems for communicating are available. These include Zoom, Discord, and Netflix Party (watching remotely together). An example is shown in Fig. 18.11. You can also attend virtual dances, online concerts, and plays. You can play many games remotely as well. People are even throwing drive-by birthday parties. Get creative on how to spend time with others without risking yourself and others to exposure.

18.11 Chatting with friends through video can provide social support.

You can hit two birds with one stone by going for a walk and catching up with a friend by phone, or walking with a friend while maintaining the recommended social distance. You can get further bonus points by walking a pet. You can also hit another two birds with another stone by asking someone for help when you need it. Friends at a distance can still provide advice, they can still provide sympathy, and they can feel better themselves for helping you, which is another useful coping strategy.

People are also turning to quarantine bubbles, pandemic pods, or quaran-teams to balance the risk of becoming infected with the positive effects connecting with others can provide us. People are figuring out ways to expand their ability to socialize with similar friends who have all agreed to abide by a set of safety guidelines and exclusivity to hang out together safely, making a quaran-team.

## Pre-existing Mental Health Conditions

Those who have generalized anxiety disorder, clinical depression, or bipolar disorder may experience an increase in their existing mental health symptoms due to the pandemic. It is vital to maintain the therapy recommended by your doctor for your mental health conditions, including therapy and prescription medication (like other chronic medical conditions). However, if your symptoms are worsening, consult your healthcare provider to see what can help you get better. The best way to socially distance and how to protect yourself might be different from recommendations for the general population.

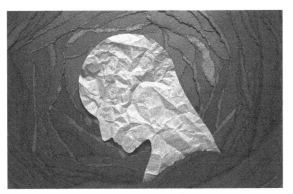

**Fig. 18.12** Mental health conditions do not go away during a pandemic, so it is important to have strategies to cope.

## If You Have Become Overwhelmed

If you feel your emotions are overwhelming you, you should consider seeking professional help. There are many options out there for you. You can reach out to your healthcare provider or therapist (if you already have one), many of whom are now offering online consultations and therapy. Do not have one? Do not worry. There are other options for you too. There are free, confidential hotlines (Fig. 18.13) available for anyone that needs it. You are not alone, so reach out if you need help. Following are just a few hotlines:

**Fig. 18.13** Crisis text lines can provide support.

| THE NATIONAL DISASTER DISTRESS HELPLINE | THE NATIONAL SUICIDE PREVENTION LIFELINE | THE NATIONAL DOMESTIC VIOLENCE HOTLINE |
|---|---|---|
| Available to anyone experiencing emotional distress related to COVID-19. | The Lifeline provides 24/7, free and confidential support, prevention, and crisis resources for people in distress. | Highly-trained advocates are available 24/7 for any victims and survivors who need support. |
| **[U18.13]** Disaster Distress Website http://disasterdistress.samhsa.gov | **[U18.14]** Suicide Prevention Website https://suicidepreventionlifeline.org | **[U18.15]** Domestic Violence Website https://thehotline.org |
| Call: 1-800-985-5990 Text: TalkWithUs to 66746 to speak with a caring counselor. | Call: 1-800-273-TALK (8255) | Call: 1-800-799-7233 or 1-800-787-3224 for TTY or if you are unable to speak safely, text: LOVEIS to 22522 |

## Summary of Looking after Yourself

Take the time to be good to yourself and know that feelings and psychological health are important to acknowledge. Emotions are normal reactions to situations. Sometimes people might say, "Do not worry." They mean well, but it could sound like you should not worry at all. Realize that whatever emotion you are having is not wrong. It is just what you are feeling at that moment. Be aware, and do not let the emotion take over. Remember, this is a temporary moment in time, and it will change. You should also remember to reach out to family and friends when you need help, social support, or someone to talk with if you need help.

**Fig. 18.14** Meditating and mindfulness can help reduce stress.

Looking after your emotional life also helps your immune response. We noted that taking care of yourself and your immune system are connected. Thoughts, meditation (Fig. 18.14), exercise, social connections, food and nutrients, and sleep all help your body's immune response. The opposite is also true: doing poorly in each area can hurt your body's immune response.

If these tips do not resonate with you, just know there are many different paths to maintaining your overall health. The best thing to do is to find tips that work best for you and weave them into your life.

**READ MORE**

**[U18.16]** Further article on looking after yourself.
[https://www.cnn.com/2020/06/02/health/natural-ways-to-improve-mental-health-wellness/index.html]

# Quiz 18: Self Care and More

This quiz is going to ask you questions about self care.

## Part 1: Stress

**Question 18.1**   Can stress be good?

A) Yes       B) No       C) Maybe

**Question 18.2**   Can stress be bad?

A) Yes       B) No       C) Maybe

**Question 18.3**   Is it ok to be scared about getting sick?

A) Yes       B) No       C) Maybe

**Question 18.4**   Is it ok to take time away from the news?

A) Yes       B) No       C) Maybe

## Part 2: Planning

Here are some questions to help you think about how to plan things into your day effectively to maintain your overall health.

**Question 18.5**   Can a routine make you feel more in control during this pandemic?

A) Yes       B) No       C) Maybe

**Question 18.6**   What should you do if you do not finish your day's planned tasks? (choose all that apply)

A) Add to the next day
B) Ask for help
C) Re-evaluate the task
D) Binge-watch Netflix until 2 AM

**Question 18.7**   Would it be helpful to list healthy meals you would like to eat for the day in your plan?

A) Yes       B) No       C) Maybe

**Question 18.8**   When planning out your activities, should you just list activities you have to take care of and do not necessarily enjoy?

A) Yes       B) No       C) Maybe

**Question 18.9**   What is the best time to plan your day?

A) The night before
B) While you are working out
C) During a Zoom call
D) While in the shower
E) Depends on your preferences as long as you plan in advance

**Question 18.10**   Is it true or false that planning can help maintain a level of normalcy in uncertain times?

A) True      B) False

## Part 3: Screen Time

These questions are about being proactive and thoughtful when it comes to screen time.

**Question 18.11**   Could changing all of your bedroom bulbs to blue light help you fall asleep more easily?

A) Yes      B) No      C) Maybe

**Question 18.12**   Can blue light help you feel more awake?

A) Yes      B) No      C) Maybe

**Question 18.13**   What can you do if you are feeling overwhelmed by the news?

A) You can take a break from the news and go for a walk
B) You can pick a couple of times a day to check in on the news for a specific amount of time
C) You can try a different source for your news
D) You can actively search for some feel-good stories
E) All of the above

**Question 18.14**   How can social media make you feel overwhelmed?

A) Spending too much time on social media and not getting your responsibilities attended to can make you feel overwhelmed
B) Sometimes, seeing others posting "perfect" looking pictures can make you feel jealous or bad about your lack of perfection and, in turn, make you feel overwhelmed by trying to attain something that might not be attainable
C) Having your phone "ding" or "buzz" constantly or have many emails to attend to can make you feel overwhelmed
D) All of the above

**Question 18.15**  Which activities can help you from feeling overwhelmed by social media? (choose all that apply)

A) Take a break and go outside

B) Try to catch up on all your social media accounts by using your phone, iPad, and computer to check three places at once

C) Set a timer when you go online to check your social media, as a reminder to give yourself a break; it is easy to get sucked down an internet rabbit hole

D) You can shut off your notifications and decide to check your email or texts when you want to, not when your notification "dings" or "buzzes"

E) You can skip meals or eat in front of your computer, so you do not miss any posts or emails

F) You can limit your connections list to connections that do not make you feel overwhelmed

G) Create a fake account with picture-perfect photos so that others can be the jealous ones for a change

## Part 4: Understanding Sensationalized Headlines

This quiz focuses on how to break down sensationalized news stories, that is, how to take the news with a grain of salt. Headlines focus on relatively rare events that we assume to be representative when they usually are not.

Some people may feel compelled to watch or read an article because the headline caught their attention. Others may want to read or watch because doubt was introduced, and they feel obliged to find out what the article states. Different readers may choose an article based on only the sensationalization of the headline and may feel baited and become frustrated with trying just to find out the facts.

We are hoping to bring awareness to this kind of marketing and help readers not to be manipulated into just accepting anything that is just written. If a reader realizes that the article they picked was clickbait, they may want to search out more information to make an educated decision for themselves about the topic they just read. Usually, with sensationalized headlines, there are small clues that indicate what is being reported is exaggerated or not completely accurate. Look at the following questions based on potentially sensationalized news headlines.

**Question 18.16**  Washington Times: "Coronavirus may have originated in lab linked to China's biowarfare program." Pick which word/group of words helps you understand why this headline needs to be read cautiously.

> **[U18.17]**  Link to Washington Times article
> [https://www.washingtontimes.com/news/2020/jan/26/coronavirus-link-to-china
> -biowarfare-program-possi/]

A) "originated"

B) "biowarfare program"

C) "may have"

D) "linked"

**Question 18.17** Fox News: "Sources believe coronavirus outbreak originated in Wuhan lab as part of China's efforts to compete with US." Pick which word/group of words helps you understand why this headline needs to be further investigated.

> **[U18.18]** Link to Fox News article
> [https://www.foxnews.com/politics/coronavirus-wuhan-lab-china-compete-us-sources]

A) "Sources"
B) "believe"
C) "Wuhan lab"

**Question 18.18** CNN: "US explores possibility that coronavirus spread started in Chinese lab, not a market." Pick which word/group of words help you understand why this headline needs to be further investigated.

> **[U18.19]** Link to CNN news article
> [https://www.cnn.com/2020/04/15/politics/us-intelligence-virus-started-chinese-lab/index.html]

A) "started in"
B) "not a market"
C) "possibility"

**Question 18.19** The Michigan Bridge, a local, non-profit newspaper, website: "Trump's coronavirus 'miracle drug' has believers. Here's what you should know." Pick which word/group of words helps you understand why this headline needs to be further investigated.

> **[U18.20]** Link to Michigan Bridge article
> [https://www.bridgemi.com/michigan-health-watch/trumps-coronavirus-miracle-drug-has-believers-heres-what-you-should-know]

A) 'miracle drug'
B) "believers"
C) "Here's what you should know"

## Part 5: Maintaining Physical Health

These questions ask you about things that can help or hurt maintaining your physical health.

**Question 18.20** Should you skip sleep and meals to reach your full potential?

A) Yes      B) No      C) Maybe

**Question 18.21** You are having a tough day. What parts of Maslow's Pyramid can you focus on that may help protect your emotional well-being? Say Yes or No, whether each activity would be useful.

A) Stay up all night listening to songs that make you cry
B) Go for a run
C) Do a guided breathing exercise
D) List things that you are grateful for
E) Withdraw yourself from others until you find another job

## Part 6: Eating and Hydration

Here are some questions about eating well and staying hydrated that help support your health and normal body functioning.

**Question 18.22**  Does eating healthily mean I cannot have ice cream?

A) Yes     B) No     C) Maybe

**Question 18.23**  Is it true that tea has a calming effect and can help you fall asleep?

A) Yes     B) No     C) Maybe

**Question 18.24**  Can you get Vitamin D from the sun?

A) Yes     B) No     C) Maybe

**Question 18.25**  If my urine is orange, am I hydrated enough?

A) Yes     B) No     C) Maybe

## Part 7: Sleep

Here are some questions about protecting your sleep that helps support your immune system.

**Question 18.26**  I am 18 now; do I still have to go to bed at the same time every night?

A) Yes     B) No     C) Maybe

**Question 18.27**  Does exercise affect sleep?

A) Yes     B) No     C) Maybe

**Question 18.28**  Does sleep affect exercise?

A) Yes     B) No     C) Maybe

**Question 18.29**  Does sleep also affect your immune system?

A) Yes     B) No     C) Maybe

**Question 18.30**  Should you stay up late for a special occasion (e.g., the last night before you or your son goes away to college)?

A) Yes     B) No     C) Maybe

**Question 18.31**  Is it a good idea to stay up late binge-watching a show?

A) Yes     B) No     C) Maybe

**Question 18.32**  Which of the following tips can help you fall asleep and stay asleep? (select all that apply)

A) Lower room temperatures to 65-75 degrees F
B) Warm bath or shower before bed
C) Watch TV
D) 4-7-8 Breathing Technique
E) Go for a run right before bed

## Part 8: Physical Fitness

Here are some questions about physical fitness during a pandemic.

**Question 18.33**  Are six exercise sessions for only 5 minutes each worth doing?

A) Yes    B) No    C) Maybe

**Question 18.34**  Is playing a team sport a good form of exercise?

A) Yes    B) No    C) Maybe

**Question 18.35**  Does walking count as an exercise if I also talk on the phone or listen to music or a podcast?

A) Yes    B) No    C) Maybe

**Question 18.36**  Should I wear a mask to exercise?

A) Yes    B) No    C) Maybe

## Part 9: Social Connections

Here are some questions about how social connections may help with your physical health.

**Question 18.37**  Can talking with a friend help with your health in general?

A) Yes    B) No    C) Maybe

**Question 18.38**  What is a "quarantine bubble"? (select all that apply)

A) A group of individuals or families whose members have been safely sheltering in place and who can now start hanging out together safely if everyone abides by the safety guidelines and agrees to be exclusive
B) A specialized bubbling sanitizer that can kill the virus in one minute
C) A pandemic pod, quaran-team, or COVID-crew (Small, strict social circles outside your immediate household whom you may socialize with, but only outside and you should still social distance, and masks are recommended)

**Question 18.39**  Is it important to connect with others?

A) Yes    B) No    C) Maybe

**Question 18.40**  Does social distancing mean you should not socialize with friends who live a distance from you anymore?

A) Yes    B) No    C) Maybe

## Part 10: Looking After Yourself

These questions are about taking care of yourself.

**Question 18.41**  Do I have to go to bed at the same time?

A) Yes    B) No    C) Maybe

**Question 18.42**  Should I worry or seek out help if I find myself crying sometimes?

A) Yes    B) No    C) Maybe

**Question 18.43**  If I do not have a psychologist or psychiatrist, am I out of luck?

A) Yes    B) No    C) Maybe

**Question 18.44**  Is it worth exercising for just five minutes?

A) Yes    B) No    C) Maybe

. . . . . . . . . . . . . . . . . . . . . . . . . . . . . . . . . . . . . . . . . . . . . . . . . . . .

**Answers to Quiz 18**

Part 1: Stress

**Question 18.1: A, Yes**
*Feedback:* Yes, stress can be a source of motivation and can help you remember to wear a mask to the grocery store, for example. However, too much stress can be bad for physical and mental health and can negatively affect your immune system.

**Question 18.2: A, Yes**
*Feedback:* Yes, high levels of chronic (on-going) stress can be harmful. It can cause us to shut down and not do what we need to do to keep ourselves safe. Excess stress can also take a toll on our health and immune system.

**Question 18.3: A, Yes**
*Feedback:* Yes, being scared can be the motivator that keeps us doing things to keep us safe. When you are so scared that you are overwhelmed and begin to shut down, then the fear has become problematic.

**Question 18.4: A, Yes**
*Feedback:* Yes, absolutely. Sometimes people just need to take a day off from all the information that seems to be endlessly thrown at us. Do something you enjoy.


Part 2: Planning

**Question 18.5: A, Yes**
*Feedback:* Yes, having a routine that includes healthy habits can help you take control of your life during these out of control times. Rather than worrying about what might happen to us, we can focus on our routine, which can include things that will help to keep us safe.

**Question 18.6: A, Add to the next day, B, Ask for help, and C, Re-evaluate the task**
*Feedback:* The best actions will involve being proactive and seeking support. Self-care is important, but try to ensure you do not compound your troubles.

**Question 18.7: A, Yes**
*Feedback:* Yes, having a healthy meal plan can help push you to maintain healthy habits.

**Question 18.8: B, No**
*Feedback:* No, you should also try to plan some time for activities you enjoy to balance your day. Engaging in activities you enjoy can benefit your mental wellbeing.

**Question 18.9: A, The night before, E, Depends on your preferences as long as you plan in advance, and possibly D, while in the shower.**
*Feedback:* The night before would be the best answer here. However, we all have our preferences. As long as you are not distracted like during a Zoom call, and you are planning in advance, it should work.

**Question 18.10: A, True**
*Feedback:* When faced with significant changes to our life and lifestyle, the stress can be tough. Maintaining some normalcy through planning will help reduce stress levels.

## Part 3: Screen Time

**Question 18.11: B, No**
*Feedback:* No, blue light can make it harder to fall asleep. If you find it hard to fall asleep, try to avoid screens or wear blue light blocking glasses two or three hours before going to bed.

**Question 18.12: A, Yes**
*Feedback:* Yes, getting blue light during the day, especially from the sun, can help you be more alert and improve your performance and mood.

**Question 18.13: E, all of the above**
*Feedback:* All of the above, all of these strategies can help you from feeling too overwhelmed by the news. It is important to check in with yourself and be proactive if you are feeling overwhelmed.

**Question 18.14: D, all of the above**
*Feedback:* All of the above can contribute to feeling overwhelmed. Be careful not to overuse social media and exacerbate your stress.

**Question 18.15: Correct Responses: A, C, D, F**
*Feedback:* Activities that take you away from social media are generally helpful. Over-stimulation (B), neglecting self-care (E), and over-use of social media (G) are all going to make the problem worse.


## Part 4: Understanding Sensationalized Headlines

**Question 18.16: C, "may have," and D, "linked"**
*Feedback:* C and D. The phrase "may have" and the word "linked" tells the reader that the information is not known for sure.

**Question 18.17: A, "Sources," and B, "believe"**
*Feedback:* A & B. In this example, the word "sources" and "believe" are both words that encourage the reader to look further into this article's accuracy. When looking through this article, the author never reveals who their source is or even what the source's expertise is. When reading any news, you should be able to locate more information that can help you determine if you believe what they are saying. They have multiple sources, but they are never named, and the article never explains why these are credible sources.
　　The next word, "believe," does not mean absolutely true, so that would be your second hint to investigate more.

**Question 18.18: C, "Possibility"**
*Feedback:* C. "possibility," again is a word that straddles a grey area, leaving the reader uncertain.

**Question 18.19: A, "miracle drug," and C, "Here's what you should know"**
*Feedback:* A & C. The quotes around the phrase '*miracle drug*' can indicate that the author does not agree with the use of the term, similar to the way we use air quotes. When quotation marks are put around a word in this way, they can be called scare quotes. "Here's what you should know" guides you to read through the whole article to find out more about the story.

## Part 5: Maintaining physical health

### Question 18.20: B, No
*Feedback:* No, according to Maslow's Hierarchy of Needs, it is harder to work on the higher levels of the pyramid if you do not take care of the foundational levels like eating and sleeping well.

### Question 18.21: No, Yes, Yes, Yes, No
*Feedback:*

A) Sleep is important, and one of the basic needs in the base of Maslow's pyramid. Sleep helps protect your emotional health, so while listening to songs and taking a moment to cry is not bad, staying up all night does not support your emotional health

B) Going for a run can help you let some steam off, and can be a great form of exercise for your overall health, and can also strengthen your mind.

C) Breathing exercises can make you feel more calm and even slow your heart rate and give you a moment to relax. Breathing is also one of the basic needs in the base of Maslow's hierarchy of needs.

D) Listing things that you are grateful for can remind you of the good things in your life and help put things into perspective when you feel overwhelmed. This is an example of a problem-solving technique that can be found at Maslow's highest level.

E) While withdrawing from others for a short period can be helpful, it is also important to remember that connections (the third level of the pyramid) are important to your emotional well-being, so you may want to reach out to a family member or friend.


## Part 6: Eating and Hydration

### Question 18.22: B, No
*Feedback:* Absolutely not! You can have ice cream. It is good to note that ice cream has some benefits too. There are vitamins and minerals in ice cream. Some even have Vitamin D, and researchers are currently testing whether Vitamin D can prevent or ease the symptoms of COVID-19. Just remember, everything in moderation, so have some ice cream but make it part of a well-balanced diet.

### Question 18.23: A, Yes
*Feedback:* Yes. Tea, particularly decaffeinated tea, is thought to have a calming effect. As research in this area is ramping up, researchers recently found drinking tea can lower levels of the stress hormone cortisol. If you are trying to fall asleep, just be sure to pick a tea without caffeine (herbal teas), such as chamomile or lavender tea.

### Question 18.24: A, Yes
*Feedback:* Yes, the sun can give you vitamin D. Remember, sunscreen blocks UVB light, so theoretically, it can lower levels of vitamin D; research is not sure how much. However, wearing sunscreen is essential as it protects your skin from sun damage and lowers the risk of skin cancer close to 50%. Overall, getting some sun every day is a worthwhile idea.

**READ MORE**

**[U18.21]**  The Lancet: Vitamin D & COVID-19
[https://www.thelancet.com/journals/landia/article/PIIS2213-8587(20)30183-2/]

**Question 18.25: B, No**
*Feedback:* No, orange urine is usually a sign of dehydration. You should drink more water.

## Part 7: Sleep

**Question 18.26: A, Yes**
*Feedback:* Yes, it helps you fall asleep and wake up more easily by maintaining the body's internal clock. Additionally, quality sleep supports your general health and your immune system.

**Question 18.27: A, Yes**
*Feedback:* Yes, exercising can help you fall asleep more quickly and can improve your sleep quality. For exercise to influence your sleep, studies have shown that people need to exercise 1-2 hours before bed for at least 30 minutes. Exercise releases the hormone adrenaline into your body, so if you exercise too close to your bedtime, it may be hard to fall asleep.

**Question 18.28: A, Yes**
*Feedback:* Yes, sleep replenishes your energy, and not having enough sleep can make it difficult to stay alert enough to exercise.

**Question 18.29: A, Yes**
*Feedback:* Yes, numerous scientific studies have found that getting good sound sleep can improve your immune system.

**Question 18.30: C, Maybe**
*Feedback:* Maybe. You might wish to stay up late on very special occasions, but generally, having a consistent bedtime schedule can help ensure a good night's sleep. Losing sleep one day probably will not change much, but it is recommended to stick to a consistent bedtime to help you fall asleep and prevent insomnia.

**Question 18.31: B, No**
*Feedback:* No, it is generally better to get a good night's sleep. Your lack of sleep may have immediate effects that you can see the next morning (e.g., you are tired), but there are effects to your immune system that are less apparent. A single day is not going to make much of a difference. It is when you make a habit of skipping sleep that it becomes a problem (for example, it decreases your immune response, increases general fatigue, and decreases the quality of mental well-being).

**Question 18.32: A, Lower room temperature to 65-75 degrees F, B, Warm bath or shower, and D, 4-7-8 Breathing technique**
*Feedback:* A comfortable temperature, relaxing activities, and purposeful relaxation will all help, whereas blue lights and high-energy activity will make sleep more difficult.

Your core temperature lowers when you are asleep, and if your room is too hot, the higher core temperature may make it harder to fall or stay asleep.

A shower or bath is the same idea as above. After you get out of the warm water, your body cools off, which may help signal your body that it is time to go to sleep.

While some people do fall asleep while watching TV, usually they are awakened by the TV and do not sleep as well.

Exercising can help you fall/stay asleep, but not right before bed. It will take a little time for your body to process the adrenaline arising from exercise, so it is best to exercise at least 1-2 hours before bed.

### Part 8: Physical Fitness

#### Question 18.33: A, Yes
*Feedback:* Yes, according to the Mayo Clinic, an average person needs about 150 minutes of moderate exercise or 75 minutes of vigorous exercise per week. If you do six moderate exercises for five minutes each (30 mins. in total per day) five days a week, you will reach your weekly exercise requirement.

#### Question 18.34: A, Yes
*Feedback:* Yes, a team sport is an excellent form of exercise. During the pandemic, the safest sports are individual sports or ones that minimize contact (e.g., tennis). However, you just have to be careful. There may be periods where team sports are relatively safe. Check the infection rate near you. In addition, during transition periods (e.g., "modified Green" in Pennsylvania), when you do participate in team sports, it may be safer to engage in an outdoor team sport instead of one inside a gym.

#### Question 18.35: A, Yes
*Feedback:* Yes, walking while talking or listening is a great way to multitask.

#### Question 18.36: C, It depends
*Feedback:* It depends. If there are people around and you are breathing heavily, then you should consider wearing a mask to reduce the chance of sharing the virus. On the other hand, WHO suggested (16 June 2020) not using a mask while exercising because a wet mask can become less effective, can make it difficult to breathe easily, and can promote the growth of microorganisms. In all cases, WHO suggests maintaining physical distance while exercising. We suggest trying to find situations where you would not need to wear a mask while exercising because it solves many problems for you. Wearing a face shield may provide some protection.

**READ MORE**

**[U18.22]** WHO FACT: People should NOT wear masks while exercising (16 June 2020) [https://www.who.int/emergencies/diseases/novel-coronavirus-2019/advice-for-public/myth-busters]

### Part 9: Social Connections

#### Question 18.37: A, Yes
*Feedback:* Actually, yes. Social support helps you feel connected and helps with general health. Friendly conversations can help reduce stress and thus improve your health and your immune system.

#### Question 18.38: A, C (see questions for the full text of answer)
*Feedback:* A quarantine bubble is a group of people who are treated as living in the same household, but may live physically in two households, but otherwise social distance and wear masks when interacting with everyone outside their bubble.

#### Question 18.39: A, Yes
*Feedback:* Yes, connecting with people is important. Your body can release the "feel-good hormone," serotonin, when you connect with others. You do not need to physically see a person to get the benefits. You can talk on the phone, or even video chat.

**Question 18.40: B, No**

*Feedback:* No, the term "social distancing" means to physically distance yourself from others to stop the spread of an infectious disease. A more accurate term would be physical distancing. Socializing is important for our mental health.


## Part 10: Looking After Yourself

**Question 18.41: A, Yes**

*Feedback:* Yes, generally, you are healthier if you go to bed at the same time.

**Question 18.42: B, No**

*Feedback:* No, feelings are a normal part of life, and you may find yourself feeling sad and crying. We are all experiencing a loss. Our lives have had major changes.

But, when you find yourself unable to find any comfort, even with some of the tips we gave, then it may be time to seek help. Sometimes, it could be a friend or your doctor, or you may want to talk to a psychologist or psychiatrist.

**Question 18.43: B, No**

*Feedback:* No, there are many options. Try some of the tips we described, and if you need help right away (24 hours per day/ 7 days per week), call the Disaster Distress Hotline at 1-800-985-5990 or text TalkWithUs to 66746. They are there to help you.

**Question 18.44: A, Yes**

*Feedback:* Yes, it is worth exercising for just five minutes at a time. More is, of course, better, but you can help your physical and mental health with just five-minute exercise sessions.

# 19

# Moving Forward and Summary Quizzes

**Fig. 19.1** COVID-19 zones. Which one are you in?

Now you know more about skills to protect yourself and your community and have moved further from the Fear Zone in Fig. 19.1 towards the Growth Zone. You should practice them as much as you can to make the skills more automatic. If we all practice these skills, we can reduce the spread of the virus and can start to get back to our normal day-to-day activities safely. Also, keep in mind, this is a new virus, and so there will be information and guidance that changes as scientists and healthcare providers learn more about the virus. Keep up to date by visiting the CDC's website—an excellent resource for trusted information [U19.1].

You should also keep up your appointments with health care providers where you are allowed. You can get ill from chronic health conditions as well as COVID-19. Check with your health care providers if you are not sure whether or not you should go to your appointment. Care for routine and chronic conditions should be continued as much as possible and practical. Appointments by phone and video may be available. Flu and other vaccines will continue to be important and helpful—get them—they are often free. When in doubt, contact your healthcare provider for advice.

To remind yourself what you have learned, you should do part 2 of the quiz in Appendix 1. Keep in mind the skills shown in Fig. 2.2 and on the back cover. Use them to stop or obstruct the pathways shown in Fig. 3.3. Where possible decrease the frequency that you are in those situations, the proximity to the potential infection sources as measured in distance or time (social distancing helps here), the duration of the time you are exposed, and the intensity of the exposure (masks help here). [U20.19]

We close with a quiz about a common activity while outside your house, going to the restroom.

Stay safe! Stay healthy! Keep up your immune system!

**READ MORE**

[U19.1]  For the latest information, see the entry page to the CDC on COVID-19
[https://www.cdc.gov/coronavirus/2019-ncov/index.html]

# Quiz 19: Summary Quiz: Bathroom Use

## Part 1: Using public restrooms safely

Here is an example scenario for you to practice your decision-making skills.

You might wish to avoid public restrooms where you can. But if you do have to go, this quiz provides a series of questions as an example story of applying the skills you have learned from this book. It touches on all of these skills. (Pun intended).

**Question 19.1**  When you go into the bathroom, should you wash your hands first?

A) Yes       B) No       C) Depends

**Question 19.2**  Can flushing a toilet infect me?

A) Yes       B) No       C) Maybe

**Question 19.3**  Can I get infected with COVID-19 from bar soap?

A) Yes       B) No       C) Maybe

**Question 19.4**  Do I have to find a paper towel or will an air dryer work?

A) Paper towel       B) Air dryer       C) Either

**Question 19.5**  What is the most dangerous bathroom item on this list?

A) Door       B) Mirror       C) Soap       D) Towel dispenser

## Part 2: Personal Activities That Can Slow the Spread of Infection

The quiz in Appendix 1 should be repeated, focusing on the second set of problems in Part 2. Now that you have completed the book, you should feel even more confident about your answers about activities that can or cannot increase your risk of exposure. Taking this quiz again will help you judge risk.

**Answers to Quiz 19**

## Part 1: Using public restrooms safely

**Question 19.1: C, Depends**
*Feedback:* It depends. You should if you are male and you have touched a dirty surface and are about to touch your genitals. If you are a woman and will not touch your genitals, you might not have to. If your hands are visibly dirty, then it would be worthwhile in any case.

**Question 19.2: A, Yes**
*Feedback:* Yes. If there is no lid or the lid is up, and there is infectious material left by someone else, then you can get exposed that way through droplets arising from flushing or previous flushing.

**Question 19.3: B, No**
*Feedback:* No, the COVID-19 viruses cannot live on bar soap.

**Question 19.4: C, Either**
*Feedback:* Either will work. A paper towel is probably safer. You might want to think ahead about how to open the door if there is one, and turning off the water if you have to do that to the water faucet. A paper towel can help with opening doors as well.

**Question 19.5: A, Door**
*Feedback:* The door, if you have to touch it with your hands to get out, you can get contaminated.

## Part 2: Personal Activities that can slow the spread of infection

See Appendix 1 for questions and answers.

# Other Resources

Here is a list of helpful resources on related topics. These resources do change with time. While showing specific information sites and tools, they also show the range of material available. These resources are available as a set at http://StopTheSpread.health/URLs.

[U20.1]   Easy to understand and use summary of cases in the US
          [Covidactnow.org]

[U20.2]   The Institute for Health Metrics and Evaluation, U. of Washington, has
          information on COVID-19, including pandemic simulations
          [http://www.healthdata.org/covid]

[U20.3]   Dr. John Campbell is a nurse educator with a series of daily updates about
          COVID-19 with advice and other nursing topics
          [https://www.youtube.com/user/Campbellteaching]

[U20.4]   Worker safety notes from The National Institute of Environmental Health
          Services (US Federal government agency, part of the National Institutes of
          Health)
          [https://tools.niehs.nih.gov/wetp/covid19worker/]

[U20.5]   The National Institute of Environmental Health Sciences COVID-19 Response
          Training (requires free registration)
          [https://niehstraining.vividlms.com/]

[U20.6]   This website notes resources from the Commonwealth of Pennsylvania. Your
          state probably has a similar site
          [https://www.health.pa.gov/topics/disease/coronavirus]

[U20.7]   This website notes resources for Centre County, PA. Your county probably has
          a similar site
          [https://covid-19-centrecountygov.hub.arcgis.com/]

[U20.8]   A comprehensive manual on how to reduce the transmission of COVID-19 in
          restaurants
          [https://momofuku.com/health-safety/sop-library/]

[U20.9]   A guide on how to talk with your children about COVID-19:
          [https://accessh.org/covidfamilyguide/]

[U20.10]  The COVID-19 solutions guide, available as a website and eBook ($16).
          It provides a broader (e.g., financial topics related to your pandemic
          experience) and somewhat shallower coverage
          [https://thecovidguide.com/book]

**[U20.11]**  A computer-based tutor that is shorter and easier to do than this material
[https://www.northeastern.edu/covid-19-how-to-be-safe-and-resilient/]

**[U20.12]**  A course (free) on how to do contact tracing
[https://www.coursera.org/learn/covid-19-contact-tracing]

**[U20.13]**  A book providing an overview of infectious diseases and how they jump
across species Quammen, David. 2012. *Spillover: Animal infections and the
next human pandemic*. New York, NY: W. W. Norton & Company.

**[U20.14]**  What to do if you have been exposed, in addition to contacting your health
care provider, Harvard Health
[https://www.health.harvard.edu/diseases-and-conditions/if-youve-been
-exposed-to-the-coronavirus]

**[U20.15]**  What to do if you have been exposed, in addition to contacting your health
care provider, CDC
[https://www.cdc.gov/coronavirus/2019-ncov/symptoms-testing/]

**[U20.16]**  A tool to predict infection rates in universities
[https://epimodel.shinyapps.io/covid-university/]

**[U20.17]**  A useful report for leaders about public health messages.
National Academies of Sciences, Engineering, and Medicine. 2020.
*Encouraging adoption of protective behaviors to mitigate the spread of
COVID-19: Strategies for behavior change*. Washington, DC: The National
Academies Press.
[https://www.nap.edu/catalog/25881/]

**[U20.18]**  An online book by Kent (2020) that has useful information in it.
[https://www.freepandemicbook.com/]

**[U20.19]**  A useful summary of what we know about COVI-19 from the US DHS.
Department of Homeland Security. 2020. Master question list for COVID-19
(caused by SARS-COV-2). Last update, 1 Dec 2020.
[https://www.dhs.gov/publication/st-master-question-list-covid-19]

# Appendix 1
## Skills to Obstruct Pandemics Quiz

## Part 1: After completing Section 2.

### Which of these can help slow the spread of infection? (Select all that apply)

**Set 1**

A. Closing the lid before flushing the toilet
B. Essential oils
C. Quarantining for 2 weeks after possible exposure
D. Washing your hands
E. Wearing gloves if your hands have cuts or sores on them

**Set 2**

A. Other people covering their coughs
B. Covering your coughs
C. Sneezing
D. Using hand sanitizer appropriately
E. Going to a large party

**Set 3**

A. Self-isolating if sick
B. Washing your hands or using hand sanitizer after using a public water fountain
C. Going into a sauna
D. Staying at least 6 feet away from people outside your home (Social distancing)
E. Not picking your fingernails

**Set 4**

A. Staying at least 6 feet away from people
B. People using masks when they are ill
C. People using masks when they do not think they are ill
D. Drinking alcohol
E. Washing your hair

# Part 2: After completing Section 19.

**Which of these can help slow the spread of infection?
(Select all that apply)**

## Set 5

- A. Taking your shoes off at the door of your house
- B. Not touching high touch surfaces
- C. Washing your fingernails
- D. Wiping down and sanitizing grocery carts
- E. Getting a haircut
- F. Getting a flu shot

## Set 6

- A. Avoiding sick people
- B. Not spending a long time in enclosed spaces with others (like a bus)
- C. Getting enough sleep
- D. Sleeping less
- E. Losing weight if overweight

## Set 7

- A. Stopping smoking
- B. Using talcum powder
- C. Not exercising
- D. Exercising
- E. Eating a balanced diet

## Correct Responses

### Part 1: After completing Section 2

#### Set 1: A, C, D, E
A) Closing the lid before flushing the toilet. [Yes]. This can help reduce the spread within households and between bathroom users.

B) Essential oils [No]. This does not interrupt the pathways of infection.

C) Quarantining for 2 weeks after possible exposure [Yes]. Quarantining after you have been exposed will help reduce the spread if you have caught it.

D) Washing your hands [Yes]. This helps if you have gotten material on your hands. Droplets and aerosols can land on surfaces, and people who are infectious (and might not even know it), could touch their nose or mouth and touch a surface.

E) Wearing gloves if your hands have cuts or sores on them [Yes]. Wearing gloves help protect your hands from being infected.

#### Set 2: A, B, D
A) Other people covering their coughs [Yes]. This helps reduce spread by limiting exposure to respiratory droplets.

B) Covering your coughs [Yes]. For the same reason as A, it is best to limit respiratory droplet spread.

C) Sneezing [No]. Though it may be out of your control, sneezing forces a large amount of respiratory droplets out, so you should be extra careful about covering your sneeze.

D) Using hand sanitizer appropriately [Yes]. This gives you additional sanitation on your hands when you are unable to wash your hands fully.

E) Going to a large party [No]. Even if you are trying to socially distance during the party, the amount of people present still increases the risks of infection.

#### Set 3: A, B, D, E
A) Self-isolating if sick [Yes]. This keeps you from spreading your infection and gives you a chance to cut off any further infections you could cause.

B) Washing your hands or using hand sanitizer after using a public water fountain [Yes]. Public fountains have lots of people touching them, so washing your hands keeps you from spreading contagions if any of those people were sick.

C) Going into a sauna [No]. Being in small, enclosed places with other people will increase the risk of infection.

D) Staying at least 6 feet away from people outside your home (Social distancing) [Yes]. This helps reduce infection from respiratory droplets by giving both people a buffer.

E) Not picking your fingernails [Yes]. Picking your fingernails leads you to touching your hands frequently, may cause holes in your skin, and may spread germs from your hands to other places.

#### Set 4: A, B, C, E
A) Staying at least 6 feet away from people [Yes]. Social distancing gives you a safe buffer zone.

B) People using masks when they are ill [Yes]. The masks reduce the spread of respiratory droplets, which are a major way that infections spread.

C) People using masks when they do not think they are ill [Yes]. Especially during an active pandemic, wearing masks regardless of illness will add additional protection from spreading and receiving infection by infectious people (asymptomatic and symptomatic).

D) Drinking alcohol [No]. Alcohol and other drugs can impair your immune system and increase the chances of an infection taking hold.

E) Washing your hair [Yes]. Washing your clothes and body will help eliminate any traces of possible contagions that could linger after being outside.

**Part 2: After completing Section 19**

**Set 5: A, B, C, D**
A) Taking your shoes off at the door of your house [Yes]. This helps keep outside contagions and dirt isolated to a smaller area of the home.

B) Not touching high touch surfaces [Yes]. High touch surfaces are a common vector for transmission, so avoiding them when possible is good risk management.

C) Washing your fingernails [Yes]. Washing your fingernails is part of a comprehensive handwashing routine.

D) Wiping down and sanitizing grocery carts [Yes]. Grocery carts are high touch objects in a high touch environment, so this is an important action.

E) Getting a haircut [No]. Any activity requiring you to get close to other people outside the household can increase the risk, but using best practices can minimize the risk.

F) Getting a flu shot [Yes]. It will help reduce influenza infections, and in doing so it will free up healthcare resources and make other infections easier to recognize.

**Set 6: A, B, C, E**
A) Avoiding sick people [Yes]. While asymptomatic people can spread the infection, sick people are more likely to be highly infectious.

B) Not spending a long time in enclosed spaces with others (like a bus) [Yes]. If it can be done, staying away from enclosed, populated spaces will reduce risks.

C) Getting enough sleep [Yes]. Sleep can help keep your immune system strong, so getting proper amounts of sleep will reduce your overall risk.

D) Sleeping less [No]. For the same reason as C, losing sleep weakens your immune system and can increase your risk of an infection taking hold.

E) Losing weight if overweight [Yes]. Maintaining a healthy weight is part of staying overall healthy, which helps your immune system respond to contagions.

**Set 7: A, D, E**
A) Stopping smoking [Yes]. Smoking weakens your immune system and can lead to infection taking hold.

B) Using talcum powder [No]. Talcum powder may dry out stuff, but will not kill viruses.

C) Not exercising [No]. Exercise is part of a healthy lifestyle that keeps your immune system operating at optimal capacity.

D) Exercising [Yes]. Exercise helps your body stay healthy and keep a strong immune system.

E) Eating a balanced diet [Yes]. A balanced diet helps your body stay healthy and respond to infections more effectively.

# Appendix 2
## Daily Activity Checklist

## TAKING CARE OF ME

### AM FEELING CHECK-IN

_____

### BASICS

- ❑ **Morning Routine**
  - ❑ Personal hygeine

- ❑ **Healthy Meals**
  - ❑ Breakfast ❑ Snack
  - ❑ Lunch ❑ Dinner

- ❑ **Vitamins**

- ❑ **Water**

- ❑ **Physical Fitness**

- ❑ **Evening Routine**
  - ❑ Nighttime hygeine

- ❑ **Sleep_____hours goal**

- ❑ **Go to Bed by _____pm**

### PM FEELING CHECK-IN

_____

### TODAY'S GOALS

_____

_____

### SOME OF THIS

- ❑ Meditation/Breathing

- ❑ Reading

- ❑ Personal Project

- ❑ Reaching Out

### LESS OF THIS

- ❑ Checking News

- ❑ Screen Time

- ❑ Social Media

- ❑ Junk Food

### TOMORROW'S GOALS

_____

_____

# Figure Sources

**1: What Does Flatten the Curve Mean?**

1.1      "Safety Match" [U1.1] by Juan Delcan & Valentina Izaguirre @Juan_delcan and Juan Delcan On YouTube [U1.2], used with permission. [https://www.youtube.com/channel/UCRjQVwyyBD2VpX2u5rFdHkw]

1.2      "Safety Match" [U1.1] by Juan Delcan & Valentina Izaguirre @Juan_delcan; Juan Delcan on YouTube [U1.2], used with permission

1.3      Image by SLH

1.4      Image by FER

**2: Summary of Flatten the Curve: The Curve Itself**

2.1      https://www.blacksburg.gov/residents/public-safety/coronavirus-covid-19-what-you-need-to-know

2.2      Image by SLH

2.3      Image by SLH using https://www.cirm.ca.gov/researchers/ipsc-repository and https://www.smchealth.org/coronavirus

2.4      Image by SLH using https://www.cdc.gov/globalhealth/stories/practice-makes-perfect.html

2.5      https://www.cdc.gov/coronavirus/2019-ncov/prepare/prevention.html

**3: Theory: Infection Theory for Application**

3.1      Image by FER

3.2      http://2015.igem.org/wiki/images/thumb/9/99/Ustchp6.jpeg/614px-Ustchp6.jpeg

3.3      https://phil.cdc.gov/Details.aspx?pid=21917

3.4      https://phil.cdc.gov/Details.aspx?pid=23311

3.5      https://www.cdc.gov/mrsa/community/photos/index.html

3.6      NIAIS image from https://www.flickr.com/photos/niaid/albums/72157625319120696

3.7      Image by SLH using FDA.gov

3.8      https://www.cdc.gov/media/dpk/diseases-and-conditions/coronavirus/coronavirus-2020.html

Q.3.15      https://fremont.gov/371/Shopping-Carts

**4: Theory: The Immune System for Application**

4.1      Image by SLH using https://www.ncbi.nlm.nih.gov/books/NBK53021/figure/ch7.f10/

4.2      Image by REJ and from https://medlineplus.gov/tears.html

4.3      Image by SLH and https://nptel.ac.in/content/storage2/courses/102103038/module1/lec1/2.html

**5: Theory: Herd Immunity**

5.1      Image by SLH corrected from https://www.nih.gov/about-nih/what-we-do/science-health-public-trust/perspectives/science-health-public-trust/building-trust-vaccines

5.2      Image modified by SLH using https://www.gao.gov/products/gao-20-646sp

**6: Social Distancing: Shelter in Place, Quarantine, and Isolation**

6.1      https://www.schriever.af.mil/News/Article-Display/Article/2120409/combat-covid-19-stress/

6.2      Colorado Department of Public Health

6.3      Image by SLH using https://www.blogs.va.gov/VAntage/70765/va-partners-covered-flu-season/

6.4      Image by SLH using https://www.phila.gov/2020-03-31-social-distancing-isolation-and-quarantine-during-covid-19-coronavirus/

6.5      Image by SLH using https://www.freepik.com/search?dates=any&format=search&page=2&query=doctor+holding+sign&sort=popular

6.6      https://www.facebook.com/MaldenPD/photos/a.786645744723343/2825010014220229/?type=3&theater

| 6.7 | Photo by Susan Spitalny, used with permission |
| Q 6.3 | whitehouse.gov |
| Q 6.4 | https://stopthespread.health/d2p2/uploaded_images/STOP_multimedia/image81.png |
| | www.whitehouse.gov |
| Q 6.6 | https://islipny.gov/news/press-releases/592-wedding-party-observes-social-distancing |
| Q 6.7 | Image by SLH |
| Q 6.8 | Image by SLH |
| Q 6.9 | https://coronavirus.utah.gov/state-clarifies-mass-gathering-instructions/ |
| Q 6.10 | Image by SLH |
| Q 6.11 | https://csi.nebraska.gov/products/seating/steel-folding-chairs |
| Q 6.12 | https://www.malmstrom.af.mil/News/Article-Display/Article/347640/commissary-hosts-deployed-spouses-night/ |
| Q 6.13 | https://www.fairfaxcounty.gov/news2/car-tax-is-due-oct-5-extended-hours-and-many-ways-to-pay/ |

## 7: Social Distancing: Not Shaking Hands

| 7.1 | https://www.casey.senate.gov/newsroom/galleries/post-exchange in May 2013 |
| 7.2 | Image by SLH |
| 7.3 | https://www.usda.gov/media/blog/2016/08/02/healthful-foods-could-be-just-click-away-fns-works-bring-online-shopping-snap |
| Q 7.A | https://wicbreastfeeding.fns.usda.gov/babys-hunger-cues |
| Q 7.B | https://www.nih.gov/news-events/nih-research-matters/warm-hands-warm-feelings |
| Q 7.C | https://www.acf.hhs.gov/ocs/success-story/x-tending-hands-strengthening-central-florida-community |
| Q 7.D | https://www.army.mil/article/217752/army_lab_industry_announce_partnership_to_develop_new_materials |
| Q 7.E | https://aderholt.house.gov/media-center/press-releases/coronavirus-resources-4th-congressional-district |
| Q 7.F | https://share.america.gov/first-lady-of-venezuela-visits-white-house/ |
| Q 7.G | https://upload.wikimedia.org/wikipedia/commons/thumb/e/eb/DapGreeting.jpg/1920px-DapGreeting.jpg |
| Q 7.H | https://www.taylorsvilleut.gov/Home/Components/News/News/198/266 |

## 8: Social Distancing: Coughing and Sneezing Safely

| 8.1 | https://upload.wikimedia.org/wikipedia/commons/thumb/7/77/Sneeze.JPG/220px-Sneeze.JPG |
| 8.2 | Image by SLH.  http://StopTheSpread.health/TransmissionSneeze.mov |
| 8.3 | Image collaged by SLH using |
| | Cough: https://www.cdc.gov/niosh/topics/asthma/symptoms.html |
| | Handshake: https://health.gov/news-archive/blog/2016/03/does-your-health-team-include-a-lawyer-attorneys-can-help-clinics-and-communities-address-the-social-determinants-of-health/index.html |
| | Hands on face: https://www.womenshealth.gov/blog/women-migraine |
| 8.4 | https://npin.cdc.gov/publication/cover-your-cough-clean-your-hands-after-coughing-or-sneezing |
| 8.5 | istockfree |
| 8.6 | https://phpa.health.maryland.gov/ Documents/ PPE%20Webinar%20Part%201%2011%2029%2018%20hs%20FINAL%202.pdf |
| Q 8.3 | https://www.cdc.gov/features/rhinoviruses/index.html |
| Q 8.4 | https://www.fairfaxcounty.gov/health/flu/cover-coughs-sneezes |
| Q 8.5 | Photo by SLH |
| Q 8.6 | Photo by MJN |
| Q 8.7 | Pixabay https://pixabay.com/service/license/ |
| Q 8.8 | Unsplash https://unsplash.com/license |
| Q 8.9 | Image by SLH based on Google search "stick figure coughing" |
| Q 8.10 | Photo by FER |
| Q 8.11 | https://www.governor.pa.gov/newsroom/gov-wolf-wear-a-mask-pennsylvania/ |

## 9: Public PPE: Overview

| 9.1 | https://www.mass.gov/news/wear-a-mask-in-public |

| 9.2 | Image modified by SLH using https://www.niddk.nih.gov/health-information/professionals/diabetes-discoveries-practice/support-behavior-change |
| 9.3 | https://www.hillsboroughnc.gov/news/news-releases/2020/4/15/625/cover-up-for-safety.html |

## 10: Public PPE: Masks

| 10.1 | Image by SLH using https://www.ncbi.nlm.nih.gov/books/NBK519802/figure/fig_unbd2/ |
| 10.2 | https://www.fda.gov/food/food-safety-during-emergencies/use-respirators-facemasks-and-cloth-face-coverings-food-and-agriculture-sector-during-coronavirus |
| 10.3 | https://www.health.ny.gov/publications/2805/index.htm |
| 10.4 | https://shopvcs.va.gov/p/49581/20-mask |
| 10.5 | https://www.cdc.gov/nora/councils/hcsa/pdfs/3-Casey-508.pdf (page 11) |
| 10.6 | https://www.lakeway-tx.gov/CivicAlerts.aspx?AID=1334 |
| 10.7 | https://www.army.mil/article/234388/sewing_to_save_lives |
| 10.8 | Image by SLH using |
| | Community giveaways: https://www.newarknj.gov/news/newark-ensures-safety-of-residents-with-free-masks-and-gloves |
| | DIY: http://www.worcesterma.gov/coronavirus/help |
| | Buy online: Photo by SLH |
| 10.9 | https://www.cdc.gov/coronavirus/2019-ncov/prevent-getting-sick/how-to-make-cloth-face-covering.html |
| 10.10 | https://www.cdc.gov/niosh/npptl/pdfs/PPE-Sequence-508.pdf |
| 10.11 | Image by SLH based on https://www.cdc.gov/coronavirus/2019-ncov/prevent-getting-sick/how-to-wear-cloth-face-coverings.html |
| 10.12 | https://ldchealth.org/442/COVID-19-2019-Novel-Coronavirus |
| 10.13 | Image by SLH |
| 10.14 | Image by SLH using |
| | Oxygen: https://www.cdc.gov/tobacco/campaign/tips/diseases/copd.html |
| | Cerebral palsy: https://www.cdc.gov/ncbddd/cp/features/cerebral-palsy-11-things.html |
| | Baby: https://wicbreastfeeding.fns.usda.gov/how-breast-milk-made |
| 10.15 | Image by SLH using https://arxiv.org/ftp/arxiv/papers/2003/2003.07353.pdf, figure s4, with permission |
| Q 10.2A | www.berkeleyheights.gov/1426/COVID-19-How-To-Help-the-Frontline |
| Q 10.2B | Photo credit, @Liz_Cheney Twitter account, used with permission |
| Q 10.2C | https://p1cdn4static.civiclive.com/UserFiles/Servers/Server_14481062/Image/News/2020/April/Articles_ACP_International_Masks_04-06-20.jpg?v=1587427200112 |
| Q 10.2D | https://eriecountypa.gov/wp-content/uploads/2020/04/How-NOT-to-Wear-a-Mask-The-New-York-Times.pdf |
| Q 10.2E | http://www.dph.illinois.gov/sites/default/files/20200331_COVID-19_Guidance_Congregate_Care_Univ_Masking_and_Env_Disinfection_Attachments.pdf |
| Q 10.2F | https://www.phila.gov/2020-04-03-how-to-use-alternative-face-masks-and-shields-for-protection-when-other-ppe-is-unavailable/ |
| Q 10.2G | https://coconino.az.gov/Gallery.aspx?PID=707 |
| Q 10.2H | https://www.hamiltonma.gov/board-of-health-order-requires-cloth-face-covering-in-stores-restaurants-starting-friday/ |

## 11: Public PPE: Eye Protection

| 11.1 | Collage by SLH using |
| | Sunglasses: https://twitter.com/DublinPIO |
| | Glasses: https://www.defense.gov/Explore/Features/Story/Article/2145366/dod-employee-sews-compassion-into-face-masks-for-coworkers-friends/ |
| | Face shield: https://www.hnc.usace.army.mil/Media/News-Stories/Article/2140231/madison-youth-joins-effort-to-help-hospital-workers/ |
| | Contact lens: https://www.cdc.gov/contactlenses/protect-your-eyes.html |

## 12: Public PPE: Gloves

| 12.1 | https://www.fda.gov/medical-devices/coronavirus-covid-19-and-medical-devices/medical-gloves-covid-19 |
| 12.2 | https://userve.utah.gov/ppe/ |
| 12.3 | https://www.cedarhurst.gov/how-to-properly-remove-and-dispose-of-gloves-masks-and-sanitizing-wipes/ |

| 12.4 | https://www.cdc.gov/niosh/npptl/pdfs/PPE-Sequence-508.pdf |

## 13: Washing: Washing Hands and More

| 13.1 | https://www.cdc.gov/handwashing/posters.html |
| 13.2 | Photo by FER |
| 13.3 | Diagram by SLH based on Taylor (1978) |
| 13.4 | Eye and Mouth: Image by AF; Nostrils: https://cs.wikipedia.org/wiki/Soubor:Nostrils_by_David_Shankbone.jpg |
| 13.5 | Images by SLH using photo by SLH and modified photo by jannoon028 on www.freepik.com |
| 13.6 | Image by AF |
| 13.7 | https://www.who.int/gpsc/clean_hands_protection/en/ |
| 13.8 | digital.gov, consumer.ftc.gov, oregonmetro.gov |
| | Left: https://digital.gov/2014/02/18/trends-on-tuesday-distracted-walking/ |
| | Center: https://www.consumer.ftc.gov/blog/2018/01/scam-spotted-thanks-clever-store-clerk |
| | Right: https://www.oregonmetro.gov/news/recycling-what-goes-bin |
| 13.9 | Collage by SLH using |
| | Door propped: https://www.firemarshal.ks.gov/DocumentCenter/View/403/Fire-Rated-Door-Booklet-PDF |
| | Door 3d handle opener: https://3dprint.nih.gov/discover/3dpx-013422 |
| | Automatic door: https://www.newhopemn.gov/city_hall/parks_and_recreation/park_construction_projects/ice_arena_entrance |
| 13.10 | https://www.uihere.com/free-photos/person-washing-his-hand-728533 |
| Q 13.6A | https://www.burlingtonvt.gov/sites/default/files/agendas/SupportingDocuments/Spec%20sheets_2.pdf |
| Q 13.7 | https://www.fema.gov/media-library/assets/images/111339 |
| Q 13.19A | Photo by FER |
| Q 13.19B | Photo by FER |
| Q 13.19C | Photo by SLH |
| Q 13.19D | Photo by SLH |
| Q 13.19E | Photo by SLH |
| Q 13.19F | Photo by SLH |
| Q 13.19G | Photo by SLH |
| Q 13.19H | Photo by SLH |
| Q 13.19I | Photo by SLH |
| Q 13.30 | https://www.osha.gov/sites/default/files/2018-12/fy10_sh-20864-10_rest_worker_manual.pdf |
| Q 13.33 | http://ndhealth.gov/ch/conference/austin.pdf |

## 14: Washing: Hand and Nail Care

| 14.1 | https://medlineplus.gov/ency/imagepages/9171.htm |
| 14.2 | Image by SLH using photo by jannoon028 - www.freepik.com |

## 15: Washing: Hand Sanitizer

| 15.1 | https://www.pexels.com/photo-license/ |
| 15.2 | Image from www.freepik.com |
| 15.3 | Image modified by SLH |
| | Using https://www.cdc.gov/handwashing/pdf/hand-sanitizer-factsheet.pdf |

## 16: Washing: Do not Touch Your Face or Mucous Membranes!

| 16.1 | https://seatpleasantmd.gov/grant-thinks-3/ |
| 16.2 | All photos source: Pexels https://www.pexels.com/photo-license/ |
| 16.3 | Image by SLH using https://health.mil/News/Gallery/Videos/2018/07/30/Fleas-2018 |
| 16.4 | https://www.airforcemedicine.af.mil/News/Display/Article/2067177/coronavirus-what-providers-patients-should-know/ |
| 16.5 | Photo by Tanino at https://www.pexels.com/ |

## 17: Washing: Objects and Surfaces

| 17.1 | https://ecology.wa.gov/Blog/Posts/January-2017/Tacoma-Smelter-Plume-New-Outreach-in-Spanish |
| 17.2 | Image from CDC |

17.3      Collaged by SLH using
Keys and cash: https://blog.mass.gov/consumer/massconsumer/doc-fee-audit/
Gas: http://ethanol.nebraska.gov/wordpress/e15-american-ethanol-blend-now-available-omaha/
Q 17.1      https://www.freeimages.com/photo/digi-lock-1241154 digi-lock-1241154-640x480.jpg
Q 17.2      Istockphoto.com COVID campaign
Q 17.3      https://www.fda.gov/consumers/consumer-updates/7-tips-cleaning-fruits-vegetables
Q 17.5      https://www.bart.gov/news/articles/2019/news20190219
Q 17.6      https://www.bart.gov/news/articles/2019/news20190219
Q 17.7      https://kingcounty.gov/depts/health/child-teen-health/child-care-health/~/media/depts/health/child-teen-health/child-care-health/documents/cleaning-toys.ashx
Q 17.8      Photo by SLH
Q 17.10      https://www.tsa.gov/blog/2016/12/15/tsa-myth-busters-did-lax-tsa-officers-prevent-childs-teddy-bear-flying
Q 17.11      https://www.energystar.gov/about/newsroom/the-energy-source/room_by_room_savings_laundry_room
Q 17.12      https://abledata.acl.gov/product/kwikset-dorian-door-lever

## 18: Looking After Yourself with the Added Benefits to Your Immune System

18.1      Image by SLH using https://www.guilfordcountync.gov/Home/Components/News/News/2029/16?selectview=1 modified from @lauraheartines
18.2      Image by SLH using https://www.nps.gov/hale/planyourvisit/sunrise-and-sunset.htm
18.3      Image by SLH using
Water: https://www.newarknj.gov/news/new-independent-water-sample-test-confirms-wanaque-system-not-affected-by-lead-issue?fbclid=IwAR0wILV7NC8wz8RPPa0v-w9p4ejlmAkGbGZCN_4m6RtiTCHO4YZncDgub0o
Veggies: https://directorsblog.health.azdhs.gov/take-the-fruits-and-veggies-more-matters-pledge/
Reading: https://blog.ed.gov/2019/06/7-tips-to-help-parents-make-summer-reading-fun/
Weights: https://portal.ct.gov/AdvocatesCorner/Life-Tips/Exercise-and-Healthy-Choices/Feeling-Good-About-Your-Weight
Timer on computer: https://www.nist.gov/image/16pml006itsinfographicfinallrjpg
18.4      Image by SLH using https://digital.gov/2016/05/23/the-content-corner-is-scheduling-social-media-posts-truly-social/
18.5      Image by SLH using images from pixabay.com
18.6      https://www.blogs.va.gov/VAntage/74005/live-whole-health-self-care-blog-9-paced-breathing-anxiety-stress/
18.7      https://www.sanjoseca.gov/your-government/departments-offices/human-resources/benefits/employee-wellness/well-being-and-covid-19
18.8      https://www.cdc.gov/nccdphp/dnpao/features/national-nutrition-month/index.html
18.9      https://p3.amedd.army.mil/performance-learning-center/sleep/sleep-and-covid-19
18.10      Image by SLH
18.11      http://www.atel.ri.gov/Deaf%20Accessibility%20Apps.pdf
18.12      https://magazine.medlineplus.gov/article/anxiety-what-you-need-to-know
18.13      https://www.nimh.nih.gov/health/education-awareness/shareable-resources-on-coping-with-covid-19.shtml
18.14      https://uk.usembassy.gov/americas-library-creates-ultimate-stay-at-home-playlist/shutterstock_658487236-3-1068x764/

## 19: Summary and Summary Quizzes

19.1      Image by SLH using https://www.maine.gov/ems/node/179

## Appendix 2: Daily Activity Checklist

Image by SLH

# About the Authors

**FRANK RITTER** BSEE PhD CPsychol is a cognitive scientist with an interest in applying cognitive science to the design of human-computer interfaces. Prof. Ritter has written or edited seven books (including Oxford, Springer-Verlag, SAGE, Nottingham) and edits a book series on cognitive models and architectures for Oxford University Press. He is an associate editor of *Human Factors*, and has been an associate editor of *IEEE SMC: Human-Machine Systems*. He helped start the College of Information Sciences and Technology, and is also a Professor of Psychology.

**AMANDA CLASE** is an Associate Research Professor in Penn State's Applied Research Lab. She has a PhD in microbiology & immunology and has studied public health preparedness and surveillance. Her research interests include biodefense, biosurveillance, infectious diseases, and global health security. Dr. Clase spent 14 years in government service designing and managing biodefense programs.

**STEPHANIE LEIGH HARVILL** is a visual design consultant with a history of working within the field of higher education and the sciences. She earned her bachelor's degree in Fine Arts and a master's degree focused in secondary education and teaching, both from UCLA. She has extensive experience helping translate science to the public in prose and figures.

**MARTIN K.-C. YEH** is an Assistant Professor at Penn State Brandywine. He has a MS in Computer Science and Engineering and PhD in Instructional Systems. He is interested in how to improve learning through technology and has helped develop the D2P tutoring architecture. He has worked on several physiology projects, including modeling the effects of caffeine with Dr. Ritter and analysing human brainwaves.

**RENUKA ELIZABETH JOSEPH** is a PhD candidate at Penn State in the Molecular, Cellular and Integrative Biosciences program, where she is researching mosquitoes-vectored viruses. She received her master of science from Johns Hopkins Bloomberg School of Public Health where she worked on anti-malarial therapeutics.

**JEFFREY OURY** is a resident physician at West Virginia University specializing in surgery. He has an MD from Indiana University School of Medicine. His research interests include infectious disease, trauma medicine, and military medicine. Prior to medicine, Dr. Oury spent more than a decade in the Army Special Forces. He served in more than 15 countries and specialized in training and cross-cultural leadership.

**ALEXIS (LEX) FENSTERMACHER** has recently graduated with a BSN degree. She worked on a trauma nursing tutor with Professors Ritter and Garrison. She is now a registered nurse on a medical surgical floor at UPMC Presbyterian Hospital.

**JACOB D. OURY** is a PhD candidate studying cognitive psychology and human-computer interaction at the College of IST at Penn State. He previously earned his BS (with Honors) in Neuroscience from the Department of Psychological and Brain Sciences at Indiana University. He is a Circle of Excellence in Teaching Support award winner from Penn State and has co-authored a book on user-centered design with Ritter that will appear in early 2021.

**EDWARD J. GLANTZ**, MBA PhD PE CISSP, is a Teaching Professor in the College of IST, Penn State. He has written a short book about how to do well at Penn State, and has written several papers with Dr. Ritter and others about disaster planning. He has taught over 13,000 students at Penn State.

**MATHIEU BRENER**, PhD, is a graduate from Penn State in Nuclear Engineering with a focus on radiation detection, remote criticality measurements, non-proliferation studies, and non-destructive analysis of nuclear material with an emphasis on neutron analysis. For a change of pace, he recently completed a post-doctoral posting in Prof. Ritter's Applied Cognitive Science Laboratory, where he helped create the STOP tutor and has co-wrote a manual for a physiology simulation.

**JAMES J. JAMES**, MD DrPH MHA, is the Executive Director of the Society for Disaster Medicine and Public Health. His doctorate is in public health from UCLA. He is the former Director of the American Medical Association (AMA) Center for Public Health Preparedness and Disaster Response. He is the former Director of the Miami-Dade County Health Department and a retired General, US Army, Medical Corps.